HOOK, LINE & SINKER

HOOK, LINE & SINKER

AN ANGLER'S COMPANION

COMPILED BY
SHELLEY KLEIN

MICHAEL O'MARA BOOKS LIMITED

First published in Great Britain in 2001 by
Michael O'Mara Books Limited
9 Lion Yard
Tremadoc Road
London SW4 7NQ

A CIP catalogue record for this book is available from the British Library

ISBN 1-85479-531-7

1 3 5 7 9 10 8 6 4 2

Designed and typeset by Design 23
Printed and bound in Finland by WS Bookwell, Juva

Lend me not to another and
I will be a quiet companion
in all your wanderings.
Wherever thou goest there
go I, through the eagle's air and over
the wide seas; through heat and cold,
calm and tempest, and the changing
years. When thou layest thyself down
upon thy bed when the weary day is
over read of me a little and thy dreams
shall be sweet; of camp sheathings and
murmuring willows, of the weir's
thunder, and the bright throats of
streams. Ye shall dream of jewelled
fishes that live in those places; of
waterfalls, brown burns, and the wild
lilies; of the freshness of morning, the
burden of noon, and that tranquil
hour when cockchafers are abroad and
owls and fishes wake to feed.

IZAAK WALTON, THE COMPLEAT ANGLER

ACKNOWLEDGEMENTS

The publisher has made every effort to contact the copyright holders of material reproduced in this book, and wishes to apologize to those he has been unable to trace. Grateful acknowledgement is made for permission to reprint the following:

'Big Two-Hearted River' by Ernest Hemingway. From 'Big Two-Hearted River', Part II. Reprinted with permission of Scribner, a Division of Simon & Schuster, Inc., from *In Our Time* by Ernest Hemingway. Copyright 1925 by Charles Scribner's Sons. Copyright renewed 1953 by Ernest Hemingway.

From *Going Fishing* by Negley Farson. Reprinted by permission of Karen Lamey.

From *Fish, Fishing and the Meaning of Life* by Jeremy Paxman, published by Michael Joseph. Reprinted by permission of David Higham Associates.

From *The Fisherman's Bedside Book* by 'BB' (Denys Watkins-Pitchford), published by Random House. Reprinted by permission of David Higham Associates.

From *Country Tales: Old Gillies* by Tom Quinn. Reprinted by permission of David & Charles Publishers.

From *Rod and Line* by Arthur Ransome, published by Jonathan Cape. Used by permission of The Random House Group Limited.

From *Gone Fishing* by Michael Hordern. Reprinted by permission of Patricia England.

From *Reflections on the Water* by Fred J. Taylor, compiled by Fred Rashbrook. Reprinted by permission of Fred J. Taylor.

'Confessions of a Rank Amateur' by Toby Buchan. Reprinted by permission of the author, and of the Editor of *Trout and Salmon*.

From *Trout Bum* by John Gierach. Reprinted by permission of John Pruett Publishing Company.

From *Still Water Angling* by Richard Walker. Reprinted by permission of David & Charles Publishers.

From *The Face of England* by Edmund Blunden. (Copyright © Edmund Blunden 1932) by permission of PFD on behalf of the Estate of Mrs Claire Blunden.

CONTENTS

From THE PLEASURES OF PRINCES

BY GERVASE MARKHAM (1614)

After a distinguished military career spanning some years, Gervase
Markham (1568–1637) became a writer on country pursuits, in
particular horsemanship, on which he wrote 'A Discource of
Horsemanshippe', published in 1593. Markham also wrote *The
Second Book of the English Husbandman* (1614), which dealt with
such matters as housewifery, husbandry, hunting, hawking and
fishing. This last was contained in the treatise, 'A Discource on the
General Art of Fishing with the Angle' from which the following
extract is taken.

Markham's precise style and obvious knowledge of the
intricacies of making rods, lines, corks and hooks reminds me of a
much later writer, John Gierach, whose obsession with tackle and
everything that 'clanks' is explored in a very humorous piece
towards the end of this anthology. That two writers with more
than three hundred years between them should resemble each
other is a good indication of just how obsessive the art of angling
can really be!

* * *

IN AS MUCH AS THE FIRST GROUNDWORK OR SUBSTANCE OF THIS ART
of angling consists in the implements belonging to it, and unless
a man is possessed of them which are most exact, nimble or
necessary for the same, his labour is in vain. For as much as the
angle-rod is the greatest, principal and sole director of all other
tools belonging thereunto, I think it not amiss to begin with choice
and order thereof according to the opinions of the best noted
anglers which have been in times past or present. For the choice
then of your angle-rod, some anglers are of the opinion that the
best should be composed of two pieces, a main body and a small
pliant top. The main body would be of a fine grown ground-

witchen or a ground-elm of at least nine or ten feet in length, straight, smooth, without knots and differing much at either end in substance or thickness. It would be gathered at the fall of the leaf and laid up in some place where it may lie straight and self-season: for to bake them in the fire, when they are green is not so good, but after they are well dried and have self-seasoned *then* bake them in the fire and set them so straight that even an arrow cannot surpass them, is excellent: then you may take the upper rind and what with the smoke and their age, their colour will be so dark that they will not reflect into the water, which is the principal observation.

Your rod having been made straight and seasoned, you shall, the upper end thereof, with an augur or hot iron, a hot iron is better, burn a hole, about three inches deep and a finger wide. Then on the outside of the rod, from the top of the hole to the bottom, you shall wrap it about with either strong double twisted thread, well waxed or pitched, or with shoemakers' thread doubled many times and well waxed with shoemakers' wax, and the last end fastened under the last fold, so closely that it does not loosen: this will keep the rod from cleaving or breaking where the hollow was made.

Having made the stock, fix the top into the hole, which would be very small ground-hazel, growing upwards from the earth, very smooth and straight, which would be cut at the latter end of the year and lie in season all winter, the upper rind by no means being taken off, neither rod put into the fire but only seasoned in a dry place, where it may lie straight and have both wind and some air from the fire to reach it. This top must be pliant and bending, yet of such sufficient strength that it will not break with any reasonable jerk, but if it is bent in any way will return to its former straightness. This top-wand would be a yard and half, or an ell at least in length, and the smallest end would be fastened with a wrap of hair, a strong loop of hair, about an inch long, to which you may at pleasure fasten your fishing line: and the bigger end of the top must be thrust into the socket of the stock and made so fast that it does not loosen nor shake out with any shaking or other reasonable violence. The witchen or ground-elm are the best to frame these main stocks, yet I have seen very good stocks made of sallow, beech or poplar: for the lighter your rod is (so be it strong) the better it is and easier to use.

There are other approved good anglers which allow only that rod which is composed of one entire piece, and think them stronger, nimbler and less casual. These rods they would have chosen are straight and well-grown ground-hazel, being from the bottom to the top finely rush-grown, the upper end being small, pliant and bending. This rod would be gathered at the fall of the leaf, when some of the leaves are fallen and some sticking: as soon as you have cut them up, cut away the leaves and small sprigs, but not so near that you hurt the bark (for that must not be stirred, as well for the strength of the rod as for the colour which being dark will not readily catch the eye of the fish and offend). Then bringing your rods home, lay them upon a level floor, and pressing them down with weights, to keep them from warping, let them lie and season all winter: then, in the springtime, take them up for your purpose, which is only to make the knots smooth and to fix your loop of hair to the upper end. Now the longest of all these rods is the best, so be it straight and well grown, for most commonly they are so short that they well serve only for fishing in little narrow brooks or else in a boat in great waters.

There are other anglers, and many of the best and approved judgements, which allow the angle-rod of many pieces: as those which are made of cane, each piece exceeding another one degree, in such even proportion that being fixed, and thrust one within another they will show as one even, and most straight rush-grown body without any crookedness or other outward evil favouredness: these pieces would not be above four foot in length and three such pieces are sufficient for the stock of the rod, besides the top, now for those ends which are the sockets into which you fix the other canes, you shall hoop them about with fine plates of brass, an inch and a half broad, well soldered and smoothly filed which will keep the cane from cleaving: and for the top of this rod, the round whalebone is thought the best and surely in my concept it is, both for this and any rod whatsoever, for it is tough, strong and most pliant. These rods most commonly are made to have small canes thrust down into the wide canes, so that a man may walk with them as with a staff and when he pleases draw them forth and use them as occasion rises: the only exception which is taken at these kind of rods is the bright colour of the cane, which reflecting into the water, often scares the fish and makes them afraid to bite. But if you fish in deep and thick waters, there is no such matter, for the shadow of the rod is not discerned through the sun, only in shallow and clear brooks it is a little hindrance and therefore he who is a master in this art will umber and darken the rod by rubbing it over a gentle fire with a little capons-grease and brown of Spaine mixed together.

Now for your lines, you shall understand that they are to be made of the strongest, longest and best grown horsehair that can be got, not that which grows on his mane, nor upon the upper part of or setting of his tail, but that which grows from the middle and inmost part of his dock, and so extends itself down to the ground, being the biggest and strongest hairs on the horse: neither are these hairs to be gathered from poor, lean and diseased jades of little price or value, but from the fattest, soundest and proudest horse you can find, for the best horse has the best hair, neither would your hair be gathered from nags, mares or geldings, but from stone horses only, of which the black hair is worst, the white or grey best, and other colours indifferent: those lines which you make for small fish, as gudgeon, whiting or minnow, would be composed of three hairs: those which you make for perch, or trout, would be of five hairs: and those for the chub or barbell, would be of seven. To those of three hairs you shall add one thread of silk: and to those of seven three threads of silk. You shall twist your hairs neither too hard not too slack, but even so as they may twine and couch close one within another, and no more, without either snarling or gaping one from another. The ends you shall fasten together with a Filbers knot, which is your ordinary fast knot, folded about four times, both under and above, for this will not loosen in the water, but being drawn together will continue when all other knots fail, for a smooth stiff hair will yield and go back if not drawn together artificially. Your ordinary line would be between three and four fathoms in length, yet for as much as there is diversity in the length of rods, in the depths of waters and in the places of standing to angle in, it shall be good to have lines of different lengths and to take those fitted for your purpose.

These lines, though natural hairs being white or grey are not offensive, yet it shall not be amiss to colour them according to the seasons of the year, for so they will least scare the fish, and entice them sooner to the bite. And of all of the colours, water-green is the best which is made in the following way: take a bottle of alome-water and put into it a handful of marigolds and let them boil until a yellow scum rises upon the water and then take half a pound of green copperas and as much verdigris, beaten to a fine powder, and put it with the hair into the water, and let it boil again and then let it cool for half a day: then take out your hair and lay it to dry and you shall see it turn a delicate green colour, which is indeed the best water-green that may be. This colour is excellent to angle with in all clear waters where the line lies plain, and most discovered, and will continue from the beginning of the spring to the beginning of winter. Now if you will have your lines of a yellow colour, you shall boil your hair in alome-water, mixed only with marigolds and a handful of turmeric; but if you cannot get turmeric, then you shall stamp so much of green walnut leaves, and mix it with the water, and steep your hair in it for twenty four hours at least. Lines of this colour are good to angle with in waters that are clear yet full of weeds, sedge and such like, for it is not unlike the stalks of these weeds, and it will well continue to angle with all the first part of the winter, as from before Michaelmas till after Christmas.

If you will have your lines of a russet colour, you shall take a quarter of alome-water, and as much strong lye, then put thereto a handful of soot, and as much brown of Spaine; and after it has boiled for an hour or two, set it by to cool, and when it is cold steep your hair in it for a day and a night, and then hang it up to dry; these coloured lines are good to angle with in all deep waters, whether they be rivers or standing pools, as ponds and such like and are most in use from Christmas till after Easter. Now if your lines are of a brown or duskish colour, you shall take a pound of umber, and half as much of soot, and seeth it in a bottle of ale, then when it is cold steep your hairs in it for a day and a night and then hang them up to dry, and the colour will be perfect, yet if you want it darker put more umber into it. These lines are excellent to angle with in waters that are black, deep and muddy, be they either running or standing water, and will continue all seasons of the year, only in bright waters are they too black, and cast too large a shadow. Lastly if you would have your lines of a tawny colour, you take lime and water and mix it together, and steep your hair in it for half a day and then take it and steep it for twice as long in tanner's ouze, and then hang it up to dry, and the colour shall be perfect. These lines are best to angle with in moorish and heathy waters which are of a reddish colour and will serve for that purpose all seasons of the year. If with this colour, or the green, you mixed a silver thread it would not be amiss, and with the other colours a gold thread is good also: and note, that at each end of your line you make a loop, one to fasten to the top of your rod being the larger, and the other to fasten your hook line unto, which would be somewhat lesser.

After your lines are made, you shall make your corks in this manner: take the best and thickest cork you can get, and with a fine razor pare it smooth and cut it in the fashion of a long Katherine Pear, big and round at one end and long and slender at the other, and according to the strength of your line, make your work bigger or lesser, as for a line of three hairs, a cork of an inch and a half in length, and as much in compass in the thickest part is big enough: and for a line of more hairs, a cork of more length and compass will become it. And indeed to speak truly for as much as it serve but only for a direction to your eye to know when the fish bites, and when you shall strike, the lesser your cork is, the better it is, and breeds less fright in the winter, in so much that many anglers will fish without any cork, with a bare quill only, but is not so certain, nor gives so sure direction as the cork does.

After you have shaped your cork, you shall with a hot iron bore a hole lengthwise through the middle and into that hole thrust a quill and draw your line through the quill and fasten both together with a wedge of the hard end of the goose-feather: and note that both your quill and your wedge be white, for that breeds the least offence in the water, then place the smaller end of your cork down towards your hook, and the bigger end towards your rod, that the smaller end, sinking down with the hook, the bigger may float aloft, and bear the quill upward, which when at any time, you see pulled down into the water, then you may safely strike, for it is an assured sign that the fish has bitten. There are other anglers which make their corks in the fashion of a Nun-gigge, small at both ends, and big in the middle, and it is not much to be disliked, only it is apt to sink sooner, and you may thereby strike before the fish have fully bitten. Others shape their corks in the fashion of a whirl, or of a little apple, round, flattish of both sides, and this cork is best of angle for the greatest fishes, because it is not so apt to sink, and will float till the hook is fastened, and the fish begins to shut away with the bait, so that a man then striking can seldom or never lose his labour.

Next to your corks are your hooks, and they are diverse in shape, and fashion, some big, some little, some in between, according to the angle at which you fish, the best substance to use is either old Spanish Needles, or else strong wire drawn as near as possible that height of temper, which being nailed and allayed in the fire, you may bend and bow at your pleasure. Now for the best softening of your wire if you make your hooks of old needles, you shall need but to hold them in a candle flame till they are red hot, and then let them cool and they will be soft and pliant enough, but if you make your hooks of strong Spanish wire, you shall roll it round and then lay it upon burning charcoal, turning it up and down till it is red hot, then let it gently cool and it will be soft enough.

Now for the making of your hooks from the biggest to the least, that is to say, from that which takes the loach, to that which takes the salmon, and let them lie before you for examples; then look what sort of hooks you intend to make and with a fine file, first make the point of your hook, which should not be too sharp for then it will catch hold of things that it should not, nor too blunt, lest it fail to take hold when needs be, therefore make it less sharp than a fine needle, and more sharp than a small pin. When you have made the point with a thin knife, you shall cut out and raise up the beard which you shall make greater or less, according to the size of the hook, and the strength of the wire: for you must by no means cut the beard so deep as to weaken the hook, but it must be as strong in that place as any other. When the point and beard are made, you shall with a pair of pliers turn and compass the hook making it round, circular-wise, somewhat more than a semi-circle, and observe that the rounder the compass the better proportioned the hook. This done, leave as much as you think convenient for the shank, and then cut it off from the rest of the wire: which done, you shall beat the end down flat and somewhat broader than the rest, and so polish and smooth it all over. Then, heating it red hot in a little pan of charcoal, put it suddenly into the water, which will bring your hook to full strength and hardness.

For single hooks, take a length of your twisted hairs, containing that number which is fit for the hook, and having made a strong loop at one end, lay the other end where there is no bough, upon the inside of your hook, then with strong red silk, either single or double according to the size of the hook being well waxed, whip and warp the hook round about as thick, close and straight as can be, in the sort of way you see men whip their bow-strings, and in the same manner make the ends of your silk fast. Then cut the silk with a pair of scissors and hairs off close by the hook, and you may be sure that they will not loosen with any reasonable force. After your hook is fastened to your line, you shall then plumb your line, by fixing certain pieces of lead, according to the size of your line about it, some being a quarter of an inch in length, some bigger,

some smaller, according to the weight of your hook and size of
your cork, for these plummets are but only to carry down your
hook, and lay it in the bottom, neither being so heavy to make the
cork dip into the water: your first plummet would be twelve or
fourteen inches from the hook, the rest not above five or seven at
the most, although some anglers use nine, and some more, as their
fancy takes them. There are several fashions of plummets used, as
one long, another, square, and the third in a diamond form, but all
tending to one end, have but one use, and the long ones are
accounted the best, so that they are neatly set to, and the ends
smooth, and closely laid down, so that they do not tangle the line
by catching on the weeds, or other trash in the bottom of the water.

Thus you have seen the best choice of rods, lines, corks and
hooks and how to fix and couple them together to do their jobs,
now we must speak of other necessary implements, which should
accompany the angler. And they are: he shall have a large musket-
bullet, through which is fixed a double twisted thread, and makes a
strong loop, which he may at pleasure hang upon his hook and
therewith sound the depth of every water, and so know how to
plumb his lines and place his corks in their due places. Then he
shall have a large ring of lead at least six inches in compass and
made fast to a small long line, through which thrusting your angle-
rod, and let it fall down into the water by your hair line, it will help
to loose your hook if it catches upon weeds or stones in the water.
Then he shall have a fine smooth board of some curious wood for
show sake, being as big as a trencher and cut battlement-wise at
each end; on which he shall fold his lines. His hooks he shall have
in a dry closed box: he shall have a little bag of red cloth to carry
his worm in and mix them with a little fresh mould and fennel:
then he shall have either a close stopped horn in which he shall
keep maggots, bobs, palmers and such like, or a hollow cane in
which he may put them and scarabs: he shall have a closed box for
all sorts of live flies and another for needles, silk, thread, wax and
loose hairs, then a roll of pitched thread to mend the angle-rod if it
happens to break, a file, a knife, a pouch with many purses in
which you can place all your many instruments. Lastly, you shall

have a little fine wanded pebbe to hang by your side, in which you shall put the fish which you catch and a small round net fastened to a pole end, with which you can land a pike or other great fish; to have also a little boat or cot if you angle in great waters to carry you up and down to the most convenient places for your pastime, is also necessary and fit for an angler. And thus I have shown you the substance of the Angler's instruments.

From THE SECRETS OF ANGLING

BY JOHN DENNYS (1613)

Little is known of John Dennys, other than that he died in 1609 and was the author of a long poem, *The Secrets of Angling*, quoted in Izaak Walton's *Compleat Angler*.

* * *

But every fish loves not each bait alike,
Although sometime they feed upon the same;
But some do one, and some another seek,
As best unto their appetite doth frame,
The roach, the bream, the carp, the chub and bleak,
With paste or corn, their greedy hunger tame,
　　The dace, the ruffe, the gudgeon and the rest,
　　The smaller sort of crawling worms love best.
The chavender and chub do more delight
To feed on tender cheese or cherries red,
Black snails, their bellies slit to shew their white,
Or grasshoppers that skip in every mead,
The perch, the tench, and eel, do rather bite
At great red worms, in field or garden bred,
　　That have been scoured in moss or fennel rough,
　　To rid their filth, and make them hard and tough.

An Anointment for Fish Bait

Recommended by M. Charras to Louis XIV,
King of France

Take of man's fat and cat's fat, of each half an ounce; mummy, finely powdered, three drams; cumium seed, finely powdered, one dram; distilled oil of aniseed and spike, of each six drops; civet, two grains; and campline, four grains; make an ointment according to art.

When you angle with this, anoint 8in of line next the hook. Keep it in a pewter box, made something taper; and when you use it never angle with less than two or three hairs next the hook, because if you do and angle with one hair, it will not stick well to the line.

From The Experienced Angler

by Robert Venables (1662)

Besides writing this treatise on angling, Robert Venables (1612?–87) was a soldier with the Parliamentary army and at various times governor of Liverpool and of Chester (he also spent a short time in the Tower).

* * *

You may also observe, what my own experience taught me, that the fish never rise eagerly and freely at any sort of fly, until that kind come to the water's side; for though I have often, at the first coming in of some flies, which I judged they liked best got several of them, yet I could never find that they did much, if at all value them, until those sorts of flies began to flock to the rivers sides, and were to be found on the trees and bushes there in great numbers; for all sorts of flies, wherever bred, do, after a certain time, come to the banks of the rivers, I suppose to moisten their bodies dried with the heat; and from the bushes and herbs there, skip and play upon the water, where the fish lie in wait for them, and after a short time die, and are not to be found: though of some kinds there come a second sort of afterwards, but much less, as the orange-fly; and when they thus flock to the river, then is the best season to angle with that fly. And that thou may the better find what fly they covet most at that instant, do thus:

When you first come to the river in the morning, with your rod beat upon the bushes or boughs which hang over the water, and by their falling upon the water you will see what sorts of flies are there in greatest numbers; if divers sorts, and equal in numbers, try them all, and you will quickly find which they most desire. Sometimes they change their fly; though not very usual, twice or thrice in one day; but ordinarily they do not seek another sort of fly till they have some days even glutted themselves with a former kind, which is commonly when those flies die and go out. Directly contrary to our London gallants, who must have the first of every thing, when hardly to be got, but scorn the same when kindly ripe, healthful, common, and cheap; but the fish despise the first, and covet when plenty, and when that sort grow old and decay, another cometh in plentifully, then they change; as if nature taught them, that every thing is best in its own proper season, and not so desirable when not kindly ripe, or when through long continuance it begins to lose its native worth and goodness.

From THE COMPLEAT ANGLER

BY IZAAK WALTON (1653)

Izaak Walton (1593–1683) was born at Stafford and later was apprenticed to an ironmonger in London whose trade he carried on, on his own account, for several years. He was a friend of John Donne, the poet, and later in life wrote Donne's biography alongside that of Sir Henry Wotton and Richard Hooker. However it is the *Compleat Angler* that has become a classic and perhaps the godfather of all 'fishing' literature. As such, no anthology on angling would be complete without it and, although some of Walton's advice might appear in today's world rather far-fetched and fanciful, nonetheless it makes for good reading. As Sir Edmund Grey, eminent statesman and fisherman, said, the *Compleat Angler* is Walton's 'best book, and I like to think it is so, because the happiness of the subject was specially suited to his kind and quiet spirit'.

* * *

*Observations of the Nature and Breeding of the Trout
and how to Fish for him*

THE TROUT IS A FISH HIGHLY VALUED BOTH IN THIS AND FOREIGN nations: he may be justly said (as the old poet said of wine, and we English say of venison) to be a generous fish: a fish that is so like the buck that he also has his seasons; for it is observed, that he comes in and goes out of season with the stag and buck; Gesner says, his name is of a German offspring, and says he is a fish that feeds clean and purely, in the swiftest streams, and on the hardest gravel; and that he may justly contend with all fresh-water fish, as the Mullet may with all sea-fish, for precedency and daintiness of taste, and that being in right season, the most dainty palates have allowed precedency to him.

And before I go further in my discourse, let me tell you, that you are to observe, that as there be some barren does, that are good in summer, so there be some barren trouts that are good in winter; but there are not many that are so, for usually they be in their perfection in the month of May, and decline with the buck. Now you are to take notice, that in several countries, as in Germany and in other parts, compared to ours, fish do differ much in their bigness and shape, and other ways, and so do trouts; it is well known that in the Lake Lemen (the Lake of Geneva) there are trouts taken of three cubits long, as is affirmed by Gesner, a writer of good credit; and Mercator says, the trouts that are taken in the Lake of Geneva, are a great part of the merchandise of that famous city. And you are further to know, that there be certain waters, that breed trouts remarkable both for their number and smallness. I know a little brook in Kent, that breeds them to a number incredible, and you may take them twenty or forty in an hour, but none greater than about the size of a gudgeon: there are also in divers rivers, especially that relate to, or be near to the sea (as Winchester, or the Thames about Windsor) a little trout called samlet, or skegger trout (in both which places I have caught twenty or forty at a standing) that will bite as fast and as freely as minnows: these be by some taken to be young salmon; but in those waters they never grow to be bigger than a herring.

There is also in Kent, near to Canterbury, a trout (called there a Fordridge trout), a trout that bears the name of the town where it is usually caught, that is accounted the rarest of fish; many of them near the bigness of a salmon, but known by their different colour; and in their best season they cut very white; and none of these have been known to be caught with an angle, unless it were one that was caught by Sir George Hastings (an excellent angler, and now with God); and he hath told me, he thought that trout bit not for hunger but wantonness; and it is rather to be believed, because both he, then, and many others before him, have been curious to search into their bellies, what the food was by which they lived; and have found out nothing by which they might satisfy their curiosity.

Concerning which you are to take notice, that it is reported by good authors, that grasshoppers, and some fish, have no mouths, but are nourished and take breath by the porousness of their gills, man knows not how: and this may be believed, if we consider that when the raven hath hatched her eggs, she takes no further care, but leaves her young ones to the care of the God of nature, who is said, in the Psalms, 'to feed the young ravens that call upon him'. And they be kept alive, and fed by dew, or worms that breed in their nests, or some other ways that we mortals know not; and this may be believed of the Fordridge trout, which, as it is said of the Stork that, 'he knows his season,' so he knows his times, I think almost his day, of coming into that river out of the sea, where he lives, and, it is like, feeds nine months of the year, and fasts three in the river of Fordridge. And you are to note that those townsmen are very punctual in observing the time of beginning to fish for them; and boast much that their river affords a trout, they exceed all others. And just so does Sussex boast several fish; as namely, a Shelsey cockle, a Chichester lobster, an Arundel mullet, and an Amerly trout.

And now for some confirmation of the Fordridge trout; you are to know that this trout is thought to eat nothing in the fresh water, and it may be better believed, because it is well known that swallows, and bats, and wagtails, which are called half-year birds, and not seen to fly in England for six months of the year, but about Michaelmas leave us for a better climate than this; yet some of them that have been left behind by their fellows, have been found (many thousands at a time) in hollow trees, or clay caves; where they have been observed to live and sleep out the whole winter without meat; and so Albertus observes, that there is one kind of frog that hath her mouth naturally shut up about the end of August, and that she lives so all the winter; and though it be strange to some, yet it is known to too many among us to be doubted.

And so much for the Fordridge trouts, which never afford an angler sport, but either live their time of being in the fresh water, by their meat formerly got in the sea (not unlike the swallow or frog), or by virtue of the fresh water only; or, as the birds of Paradise and the chameleon are said to live, by the sun and the air.

There is also in Northumberland a trout called a bull-trout, of a much greater length and bigness than any in the southern parts. And there are, in many rivers that relate to the sea, salmon-trouts, as much different from others, both in shape and in their spots, as we see sheep in some countries differ one from another in their shape and bigness, and in the fineness of their wool: and, certainly as some pastures breed larger sheep, so do some rivers, by reason of the ground over which they run, breed larger trouts.

Now the next thing that I will commend to your consideration is, that the trout is of a more sudden growth than other fish. Concerning which, you are also to take notice, that he lives not so long as the perch, and divers other fishes do, as Sir Francis Bacon hath observed in his *History of Life and Death*.

And next you are to take notice, that he is not like the crocodile, which if he lives never so long, yet always thrives till his death; but it is not so with the trout, for after he has come to his full growth, he declines in his body, and keeps his bigness, or thrives only in his head till his death. And you are to know, that he will about, especially before, the time of his spawning, get almost miraculously through weirs and flood-gates against the streams; even through such high and swift places as is almost incredible. Next, that the trout usually spawns about October or November, but in some rivers a little sooner or later: which is the more observable, because most other fish spawn in the spring or summer, when the sun hath warmed both the earth and the water, and made it fit for generation. And you are to note that he continues many months out of season; for it may be observed of the trout, that he is like the buck or the ox, that he will not be fat in many months, though he go in the very same pasture that horses do, which will be fat in one month: and so you may observe that most other fishes recover strength, and grow sooner fat and in season than the trout doth.

And next you are to note, that till the sun gets to such a height as to warm the earth and the water, the trout is sick and lean, and lousy, and unwholesome: for you shall in winter find him to have a big head, and then to be lank, and thin, and lean: at which time many of them have sticking on the sugs, or trout-lice, which is a kind of worm, in shape like a clove or pin, with a big head, and stick close to him and sucks his moisture; those, I think, the trout breeds himself, and never thrives till he free himself from them, which is when warm weather comes; and then, as he grows stronger, he gets from the dead, still water, into the sharp stream, and there lies at the watch for any fly or minnow that comes near to him; and he especially loves the May-fly, which is bred of the codworm or cadis; and these make the trout bold and lusty, and he is usually fatter and better meat at the end of that month than at any time of the year.

Now you are to know that it is observed, that usually the best trouts are either red or yellow; though some (as the Fordridge trout) be white and yet good; but that is not usual: and it is a note observable, that the female trout hath usually a less head, and a deeper body than the male trout, and is usually the better meat. And note, that a hog-back and a little head to either trout, salmon, or any other fish, is a sign that that fish is in season. But yet you are to note, that as you see some willows or palm trees bud and blossom sooner than others do, so some trouts be, in rivers, sooner in season: and as some hollies or oaks are longer before they cast their leaves, so are some trouts in rivers longer before they go out of season.

And you are to note, that there are several kinds of trouts: but these several kinds are not considered but by very few men; for they go under the general name of trouts; just as pigeons do, in most places; though, it is certain, there are tame and wild pigeons; and of the tame, there be helmets and runts, and carriers and croppers; and indeed too many to name. Nay, the Royal Society have found published lately, that there be thirty and three kinds of spiders; and yet all (for aught I know) go under that one general name of spider. And it is so with many kinds of fish, and of trouts especially; which differ in their bigness and shape and spots and colour. The great Kentish hens may be an instance, compared to other hens. And, doubtless, there is a kind of small trout, which will never thrive to be big; that breeds very many more than others do, that be of a larger size: which you may rather believe, if you consider that the little wren and titmouse will have twenty young ones at a time, when usually the noble hawk, or the musical thrassel or blackbird, exceed not four or five.

And now you shall see me try my skill to catch a trout; and at my next walking, either this evening or tomorrow morning, I will give you direction how you yourself shall fish for him.

Ven. [*Venator*, Latin for 'hunter'] Trust me, master, I see now it is a harder matter to catch a trout than a chub: for I have put on patience, and followed you these two hours, and not seen a fish stir, neither at your minnow nor your worm.

Pisc. [*Piscator*, Latin for 'fisherman'] Well, scholar, you must endure worse luck sometime, or you will never make a good angler. But what say you now? There is a trout now, and a good one too, if I can but hold him, and two or three more turns will tire him. Now you see he lies still, and the sleight is to land him. Reach me that landing net; so, sir, now he is mine own, what say you now? Is not this worth all my labour and your patience?

Ven. On my word, master, this is a gallant trout; what shall we do with him?

Pisc. Marry, e'en eat him to supper; we'll go to my hostess, from whence we came; she told me, as I was going out of door, that my brother Peter, a good angler and a cheerful companion, had sent word that he would lodge there tonight, and bring a friend with him. My hostess has two beds, and I know you and I may have the best; we'll rejoice with my brother Peter and his friend, tell tales, or sing ballads, or make a catch, or find some harmless sport to content us and pass away a little time, without offence to God or man.

Ven. A match, good master, let's go to that house; for the linen looks white, and smells of lavender, and I love to lie in a pair of sheets that smell so. Let's be going, good master, for I am hungry again with fishing.

Pisc. Nay, stay a little, good scholar; I caught my last trout with a worm; now I will put on a minnow, and try a quarter of an hour about yonder trees for another; and so walk towards our lodging. Look you, scholar, thereabout we shall have a bite presently or not at all. Have with you, sir! o' my word I have hold of him. Oh! it is a great logger-headed chub; come hang him upon that willow twig, and let's be going. But turn out of the way a little, good scholar, towards yonder high honeysuckle hedge; there we'll sit and sing, whilst this shower falls so gently upon the teeming earth, and gives yet a sweeter smell to the lovely flowers that adorn these verdant meadows.

Look! under that broad beech tree I sat down when I was last this way a-fishing. And the birds in the adjoining grove seemed to have a friendly contention with an echo, whose dead voice seemed to live in a hollow tree, near to the brow of that primrose hill. There I sat viewing the silver streams glide silently towards their centre, the tempestuous sea; yet sometimes opposed by rugged roots and pebble-stones, which broke their waves and turned them into foam. And sometimes I beguiled time by viewing the harmless lambs; some leaping securely in the cool shade, whilst others sported themselves in the cheerful sun; and saw others craving comfort from the swollen udders of their bleating dams. As I thus sat, these other sights had so fully possessed by soul with content, that I thought, as the poet hath happily expressed it,

> I was for that time lifted above the earth,
> And possess'd joys not promised in my birth.

More Directions how to Fish for, and how to make for the Trout on Artificial Minnow and Flies; with some Merriment.

THE TROUT IS USUALLY CAUGHT WITH A WORM OR A MINNOW (which some call a penk) or with a fly, viz., either a natural or an artificial fly: concerning which three I will give you some observations and directions.

And, first, for worms: of these there be very many sorts: some breed only in the earth, as the earthworm; others of or

amongst plants, as the dung-worm; and others breed either out of excrements or in the bodies of living creatures, as in the horns of sheep or deer; or some of dead flesh, as the maggot or gentle, and others.

Now these be most of them particularly good for particular fishes: but for the trout, the dew-worm (which some also call the lob-worm) and the brandling are the chief; and especially the first for a great trout, and the latter for a less. There be also of lob-worms some called squirrel-tails (a worm that has a red head, a streak down the back, and a broad tail) which are noted to be the best, because they are the toughest and most lively, and live longest in the water: for you are to know that a dead worm is but a dead bait, and like to catch nothing, compared to a lively, quick, stirring worm: and for a brandling, he is usually found in an old dunghill, or some very rotten place near to it: but most usually in cow-dung or hog's dung, rather than horse-dung, which is somewhat too hot and dry for that worm. But the best of them are to be found in the bark of the tanners, which they cast up in heaps after they have used it about their leather.

There are also divers other kinds of worms, which for colour and shape alter even as the ground out of which they are got; as the marsh-worm, the tag-tail, the dock-worm, the oak-worm, the gilt-tail, the twachel, or lob-worm, which of all others is the most excellent bait for salmon; and too many to name, even as many sorts as some think there be of several herbs or shrubs, or of several kinds of birds in the air; of which I shall say no more, but tell you that what worms soever you fish with are better for being well scoured, that is, long kept before they be used: and in case you have not been provident, then the way to cleanse and scour them quickly is to put them all night in water, if they be lob-worms, and then you put them into your bag with fennel. But you must not put your brandlings above an hour in water, and then put them into fennel, for sudden use: but if you have time, and purpose to keep them long, then they be best preserved in an earthen pot, with good store of moss, which is to be fresh every three or four days in summer, and every week or eight days in winter; or, at least, the moss taken from them and clean washed, and wrung betwixt your hands till it be dry, and then put it to them again. And when your worms, especially the brandling, begins to be sick and lose of his bigness, then you may recover him by putting a little milk or cream (about a spoonful in a day) into them, by drops on the moss; and if there be added to the cream an egg beaten and boiled in it, then it will both fatten and preserve them long. And note, that when the knot, which is near to the middle of the brandling, begins to swell, then he is sick; and, if he be not well looked to, is near dying. And for moss, you are to note, that there be divers kinds of it, which I could name to you, but I will only tell you that that which is likest a buck's-horn is the best except it be soft white moss, which grows on some heaths, and is hard to be found. And note, that in a very dry time, when you are put to an extremity for worms, walnut tree leaves squeezed into water, or salt in water, to make it bitter or salt, and then that poured on the ground, where you shall see worms are used to rise in the night, will make them to appear above the ground presently. And you may take notice, some say that camphor, put into your bag with your moss and worms, gives them a strong and so tempting a smell, that the fish fare the worse and you the better for it.

And now I shall show you how to bait your hook with a worm, so as shall prevent you from much-trouble, and the loss of many a hook too, when you fish for a trout with a running-line, that is to say, when you fish for him by hand at the ground: I will direct you in this as plainly as I can, that you may not mistake.

Suppose it be a big lob-worm, put your hook into him somewhat above the middle, and out again a little below the middle; having so done, draw your worm above the arming of your hook: but note that at the entering of your hook it must not be at the head-end of the worm, but at the tail-end of him, and having drawn him above the arming of your hook, then put the point of your [hook?] again into the very head of the worm, till it come near to the place where the point of the hook first came out: and then draw back that part of the worm that was above the shank or arming of your hook, and so fish with it. And if you mean to fish with two worms, then put the second on before you turn back the hook's-head of the first worm: you cannot lose above two or three worms before you attain to what I direct you; and having attained it, you will find it very useful, and thank me for it, for you will run on the ground without tangling.

Now for the Minnow or Penk: he is not easily found and caught till March, or in April, for then he appears first in the river; nature having taught him to shelter and hide himself, in the winter, in ditches that be near to the river; and there both to hide, and keep himself warm, in the mud, or in the weeds, which rot not so soon as in a running river, in which place if he were in winter, the distempered floods that are usually in that season would suffer him to take no rest, but carry him headlong to mills and weirs, to his confusion. And of these minnows; first you are to know that the biggest size is not the best; and next, that the middle size and the whitest are the best; and then you are to know, that your minnow must be so put on your hook, that it must turn round when 'tis drawn against the stream; and, that it may turn nimbly, you must put it on a big-sized hook, as I shall now direct you, which is thus: put your hook in at his mouth, and out at his gill; then, having drawn your hook two or three inches beyond or through his gill, put it again into his mouth, and the point and beard out at his tail; and then tie the hook and his tail about, very neatly, with a white thread, which will make it the apter to turn quick in the water: that done, pull back that part of your line which was slack when you did put your hook into the minnow the second time; I say, pull that part of your line back, so that it shall fasten the head, so that the body of the minnow shall be almost straight on your hook: this done, try how it will turn, by drawing it across the water or against the stream; and if it do not turn nimbly, then turn the tail a little to the right or left hand, and try again, till it turn quick; for if not, you are in danger to catch nothing: for know, that in case you want a minnow, then a small loach or a stickle-bag, or any other small fish that will turn quick, will serve as well: and you are yet to know, that you may salt them, and by that means keep them ready and fit for use three or four days or longer; and that of salt, bay-salt is the best.

And here let me to tell you, what many old anglers know right well, that at some times, and some waters, a minnow is not to be got; and therefore let me tell you, I have (which I will show you) an artificial minnow, that will catch a trout as well as an artificial fly, and it was made by a handsome woman that had a fine hand, and a live minnow lying by her: the mould or body of the minnow was cloth, and wrought upon or over it thus with a needle: the back of it with very sad French green silk, the paler green silk towards the belly, shadowed as perfectly as you can imagine, just as you see a minnow; the belly was wrought also with a needle, and it was a part of it white silk, and another part of it with silver thread; the tail and fins were of a quill which was shaven thin; the eyes were of two little black beads, and the head was so shadowed, and all of it so curiously wrought, and so exactly dissembled that it would beguile any sharp-sighted trout in a swift stream. And this minnow I will now show you; look, here it is, and, if you like it, lend it you, to have two or three made by it; for they be easily carried about an angler, and be of excellent use; for note, that a large trout will come as fiercely at a minnow as the highest mettled hawk doth seize on a partridge, or a greyhound on a hare. I have been told that a hundred and sixty minnows have been found in a trout's belly; either the trout had devoured so many, or the miller that gave it to a friend of mine had forced them down his throat after he had taken him.

Now for flies, which is the third bait wherewith trouts are usually taken. You are to know that there are so many sorts of flies as there be of fruits: I will name you but some of them; as the dun-fly, the stone-fly, the red-fly, the moor-fly, the tawny-fly, the shell-fly, the cloudy or blackish-fly, the flag-fly, the vine-fly; there be of flies, caterpillars, and canker-flies, and bear-flies; and indeed too many either for me to name, or for you to remember: and their breeding is so various and wonderful, that I might easily amaze myself, and tire you in a relation of them.

And, yet, I will exercise your promised patience by saying a little of the caterpillar, or the palmer-fly or worm; that by them you may guess what a work it were, in a discourse, but to run over those many flies, worms, and little living creatures with which the sun and summer adorn and beautify the river-banks and meadows, both of the recreation and contemplation of us anglers; pleasures which, I think, I myself enjoy more than any other man that is not of my profession.

Pliny holds an opinion that many have their birth or being from a dew that in the spring falls from the leaves of the trees; and that some kinds of them are from a dew left upon herbs or flowers; and others, from a dew left upon coleworts or cabbages: all which kinds of dew being thickened and condensed, are by the sun's generative heat most of them hatched, and in three days made living creatures; and these of several shapes and colours; some being hard and tough, some smooth and soft; some are horned in their head, some in their tail, some have none; some have hair, some none; some have sixteen feet, some less, and some have none; but (as our Topsel hath with great diligence observed) those which have none move upon the earth, or upon broad leaves, their motion being not unlike to the waves of the sea. Some of them, he also observes, to be bred of the eggs of other caterpillars, and that those in their time turn to be butterflies; and again, that their eggs turn the following year to be caterpillars. And some affirm that every plant has his particular fly or caterpillar, which it breeds and feeds. I have seen, and may therefore affirm it, a green caterpillar or worm, as big as a small peascod, which had fourteen legs, eight on the belly, four under the neck, and two near the tail. It was found on a hedge of privet, and was taken thence and put into a large box, and a little branch or two of privet put to it, on which I saw it feed as sharply as a dog gnaws a bone; it lived thus five or six days, and thrived and changed the colour two or three times; but by some neglect in the keeper of it, it then died, and did not turn to a fly: but if it had lived, it had doubtless turned to one of those flies that some call flies of prey, which those that walk by the rivers may, in summer, see fasten on smaller flies, and, I think, make them their food. And 'tis observable, that as there be these flies of prey, which be very large, so there be others, very little, created, I think, only to feed them, and breed out of I know not what; whose life, they say, nature intended not to exceed an hour: and yet that life is thus made shorter by other flies, or by accident.

It is needless to tell you what the curious searchers into nature's productions have observed of these worms and flies: but yet I shall tell you what Aldrovandus, our Topsel, and others say of the palmer-worm, or caterpillar, that whereas others content themselves to feed on particular herbs or leaves (for most think those very leaves that gave them life and shape give them a particular feeding and nourishment, and that upon them they usually abide) yet he observes that this is called a pilgrim, or palmer-worm, for his very wandering life and various food: not contenting himself, as others do, with any one certain place for his abode, nor any certain kind of herb or flower for his feeding, but will boldly and disorderly wander up and down, and not endure to be kept to a diet, or fixed to a particular place.

Nay, the very colours of caterpillars are, as one has observed, very elegant and beautiful. I shall (for a taste of the rest) describe one of them; which I will, sometimes the next month, show you feeding on a willow tree; and you shall find him punctually to answer this very description: his lips and mouth somewhat yellow;

his eyes black as jet; his forehead purple; his feet and hinder parts green; his tail two-forked and black; the whole body stained with a kind of red spots, which run along the neck and shoulder-blade, not unlike the form of St Andrew's cross, or the letter X, made thus cross-wise, and a white line drawn down his back to his tail; all which add much beauty to his whole body. And it is to me observable, that at a fixed age this caterpillar gives over to eat, and towards winter comes to be covered over with a strange shell or crust, called an aurelia: and so lives a kind of dead life, without eating, all the winter; and, as others of several kinds turn to be several kinds of flies and vermin the spring following, so this caterpillar then turns to be a painted butterfly.

Come, come, my scholar, you see the river stops our morning walk, and I will also here stop my discourse . . .

From Rural Sports

by John Gay (1713)

John Gay (1685–1732) is perhaps best known for *The Beggar's Opera*, which met with remarkable success in 1728 and is still performed to this day. However his career was not always so illustrious. He was secretary to the Duchess of Monmouth during which time he wrote *Rural Sports*, from which this poem is taken, but later on he speculated disastrously with the proceeds from his poems in South Sea Funds and his hopes of advancement were ruined. He died in 1732 and was buried in Westminster Abbey. On his monument is inscribed the epitaph written by himself:

> Life is a jest, and all things show it;
> I thought so once, and now I know it.

You must not ev'ry worm promiscuous use,
Judgement will tell thee proper bait to choose;
The worm that draws a long immod'rate size
The trout abhors, and the rank morsel flies;
And if too small, the naked fraud's in sight,
And fear forbids, while hunger does invite.
Those baits will best reward the fisher's pains,
Whose polish'd tails a shining yellow stains;
Cleanse them from filth, to give a tempting gloss,
Cherish the sullied reptile race with moss;
Amid the verdant bed they twine, they toil,
And from their bodies wipe their native soil.

From THE ART OF ANGLING

BY RICHARD BROOKES (1790)

THE CARP GROWS SOMETIMES TO THE LENGTH OF A YARD AND A half, and a proportionate thickness. In 1739, a pretty large one was caught in the Thames, near Hampton Court, which weighed thirteen pounds. Willoughby affirms that the largest weigh twenty pounds. The colour of this fish, especially when full-grown, is yellow; the scales are large, the head short, and like that of a tench; the mouth is of a middle size; the lips flat, fleshy, and yellow. It is without teeth, but there is a triangular bone in the palate and two other bones in the throat, which serve the same purpose. On the upper lip, near the corner of the mouth, are two yellow appendages, which may be called mustachios, from their situation. The fins are large; the tail is straight, and passes through the middle of each side.

It has no tongue, but in the room thereof nature has provided a fleshy palate, which being taken out of the mouth looks like a tongue, and some persons pretend to be positive that it is one.

Some imagine it is only the small carp that are the breeders, but this is a mistake. A gentleman in Cheshire cleansed his moat, and stored it with large carp, imagining, as the larger sort did not breed, they would feed well; but, in a very small time, the moat was all alive with carp spawn.

They spawn several times a year, but the principal are in May and August, in which months they are lean and insipid, and swim along, and are generally followed by thirteen or fourteen males who impregnate it as it falls, yet a great deal of it perishes. They are said to live to a great age, and to spawn from two years old to thirty.

One thing observable in a carp is, that it lives the longest out of water of any other fish; and Mr Derham assures us, that in Holland they hang them up in cellars, or other cool places, in a small net, full of wet moss, with only their heads out, and feed them with white bread soaked in milk for many days.

A FEW CHOICE WORDS FROM
SAMUEL JOHNSON

Fly fishing may be a very pleasant amusement; but angling or float fishing I can only compare to a stick and a string, with a worm at one end and a fool at the other.

From THE EXCURSION

BY WILLIAM WORDSWORTH (1814)

William Wordsworth (1770–1850) will always be known as the man who wrote a poem on daffodils. However, his work was very wide-ranging and, alongside Coleridge, Byron and Shelley, he became known as one of the great Romantic poets. *The Excursion*, which was published in 1814, was to have been the middle section of a three-part piece 'on man, on nature and on human life'. This small extract is particularly beautiful. I can almost see those 'crimson-spotted trouts' and the proud mien of the two companion anglers.

* * *

'A blessed lot is yours!'
He said, and with that exclamation breathed
A tender sigh;– but, suddenly the door
Opening, with eager haste two lusty Boys
Appeared – confusion checking their delight.
– Not Brothers they in feature or attire;
But fond Companions, so I guessed, in field
And by the river-side – from which they come,
A pair of Anglers, laden with their spoil.
One bears a willow-pannier on his back,

The Boy of plainer garb, and more abashed
In countenance, – more distant and retired.
Twin might the Other be to that fair Girl
Who bounded tow'rds us from the garden mount.
Triumphant entry this to him! – for see,
Between his hands he holds a smooth blue stone,
On whose capacious surface is outspread
Large store of gleaming crimson-spotted trouts;
Ranged side by side, in regular ascent,
One after one, still lessening by degree
Up to the dwarf that tops the pinnacle.
Upon the Board he lays the sky-blue stone
With its rich spoil: their number he proclaims;
Tells from what pool the noblest had been dragged;
And where the very monarch of the brook,
After long struggle, had escaped at last –
Stealing alternately at them and us
(As doth his Comrade too) a look of pride.
And, verily, the silent Creatures made
A splendid sight together thus exposed;
Dead – but not sullied or deformed by Death,
That seemed to pity what he could not spare.
But oh! the animation in the mien
Of those two Boys! Yea in the very words
With which the young Narrator was inspired,
When, as our questions led, he told at large
Of that day's prowess! Him might I compare,
His look, tones, gestures, eager eloquence,
To a bold Brook which splits for better speed,
And, at the self-same moment, ever and anon
Parted and reunited: his Compeer
To the still Lake, whose stillness is to the eye
As beautiful, as grateful to the mind.

From WALDEN; OR LIFE IN THE WOODS

BY HENRY THOREAU (1854)

Henry Thoreau (1817–62) devoted his life to literary pursuits, supporting himself by school-teaching and later on by surveying, but in 1845, in search of the simple life, he left his home in Concord, Massachusetts and built himself a cabin on Walden Pond. There he lived for more than two years, observing and communing with nature whilst also writing a journal. The journal, of course, turned out to be his most famous book and no fishing anthology would be complete without including Thoreau's account of fishing on Walden Pond. It's a beautiful piece, describing as it does the lake, the surrounding woods and the abundant wildlife.

* * *

OCCASIONALLY, AFTER MY HOEING WAS DONE FOR THE DAY, I joined some impatient companion who had been fishing on the pond since morning, as silent and motionless as a duck or a floating leaf, and, after practising various kinds of philosophy, had concluded commonly, by the time I arrived, that he belonged to the ancient sect of Cenobites. There was one older man, an excellent fisher and skilled in all kinds of woodcraft, who was pleased to look upon my house as a building erected for the convenience of fishermen; and I was equally pleased when he sat in my doorway to arrange his lines. Once in a while we sat together on the pond, he at one end of the boat, and I at the other; but not many words passed between us, for he had grown deaf in his later years, but he occasionally hummed a psalm, which harmonized well enough with my philosophy. Our intercourse was thus altogether one of unbroken harmony, far more pleasing to remember than if it had been carried on by speech. When, as was

commonly the case, I had none to commune with, I used to raise
the echoes by striking a paddle on the side of my boat, filling the
surrounding woods with circling and dilating sound, stirring them
up as the keeper of a menagerie his wild beasts, until I elicited a
growl from every wooded vale and hillside.

In warm evenings I frequently sat in the boat playing the flute,
and saw the perch, which I seem to have charmed, hovering around
me, and the moon traveling over the ribbed bottom, which was
strewed with the wrecks of the forest. Formerly I had come to this
pond adventurously, from time to time, in dark summer nights,
with a companion, and making a fire close to the water's edge,
which we thought attracted the fishes, we caught pouts with a
bunch of worms strung on a thread, and when we had done, far in
the night, threw the burning brands high into the air like
skyrockets, which, coming down into the pond, were quenched
with a loud hissing, and we were suddenly groping in total
darkness. Through this, whistling a tune, we took our way to the
haunts of men again. But now I had made my home by the shore.

Sometimes, after staying in a village parlor till the family had
all retired, I have returned to the woods, and, partly with a view to
the next day's dinner, spent the hours of midnight fishing from a
boat by moonlight, serenaded by owls and foxes, and hearing, from
time to time, the creaking note of some unknown bird close at
hand. These experiences were very memorable and valuable to me,
anchored in forty feet of water, and twenty or thirty rods from the
shore, surrounded sometimes by thousands of small perch and
shiners, dimpling the surface with their tails in the moonlight, and
communicating by a long flaxen line with mysterious nocturnal
fishes which had their dwelling forty feet below, or sometimes
dragging sixty feet of line about the pond as I drifted in the gentle
night breeze, now and then feeling a slight vibration along it,
indicative of some life prowling about its extremity, of dull
uncertain blundering purpose there, and slow to make up its mind.
At length you slowly raise, pulling hand over hand, some horned
pout squeaking and squirming to the upper air. It was very queer,
especially in dark nights, when your thoughts had wandered to vast

and cosmogonal themes in other spheres, to feel this faint jerk, which came to interrupt your dreams and link you to Nature again. It seemed as if I might next cast my line upward into the air, as well as downward into this element, which was scarcely more dense. Thus I caught two fishes as it were with one hook.

* * *

THE SCENERY OF WALDEN IS ON A HUMBLE SCALE AND, THOUGH very beautiful, does not approach to grandeur, nor can it much concern one who had not long frequented it or lived by its shore; yet this pond is remarkable for its depth and purity to merit a particular description. It is a clear and deep green well, half a mile long and a mile and three quarters in circumference, and contains about sixty-one and a half acres; a perennial spring in the midst of pine and oak woods, without any visible inlet or outlet except by the clouds and evaporation. The surrounding hills rise abruptly from the water to the height of forty to eighty feet, though on the southeast and east they attain to about one hundred and one hundred and fifty feet respectively, within a quarter and a third of a mile. They are exclusively woodland. All our Concord waters have two colors at least; one when viewed at a distance, and another, more proper, close at hand. The first depends more on the light, and follows the sky. In clear weather, in summer, they appear blue at a little distance, especially if agitated, and at a great distance all appear alike. In stormy weather they are sometimes of a slate color. The sea, however, is said to be blue one day and green another without any perceptible change in the atmosphere. I have seen our river, when, the landscape being covered with snow, both water and ice were almost as green as grass. Some consider blue 'to be the color of pure water, whether liquid or solid.' But, looking directly down into our waters from a boat, they are seen to be of very different colors. Walden is blue at one time and green at another, even from the same point of view. Lying between the earth and the heavens, it partakes of the color of both. Viewed from a hilltop it reflects the color of the sky; but near at hand it is of a yellowish tint next the shore where you can see the sand, then a light green, which gradually deepens to a uniform dark green in the body of the pond. In some lights, viewed from a hilltop, it is of a vivid green next the shore. Some have referred to the reflection of the verdure; but it is equally green there against the railroad sand-bank, and in the spring, before the leaves are expanded, and it may be simply the result of the prevailing blue mixed with the yellow of the sand. Such is the color of its iris. This is that portion, also, where in the spring, the ice being warmed by the heat of the sun reflected from the bottom, and also transmitted through the earth, melts first and forms a narrow canal about the still frozen middle. Like the rest of our waters, when much agitated, in clear weather, so that the surface of the waves may reflect the sky at the right angle, or because there is more light mixed with it, it appears at a little distance of a darker blue than the sky itself; and at such a time, being on its surface, and looking with divided vision, so as to see the reflection, I have discerned a matchless and indescribable light blue, such as watered or changeable silks and sword blades suggest, more cerulean than the sky itself, alternating with the original dark green on the opposite side of the waves, which last appeared but muddy in comparison. It is a vitreous greenish blue, as I remember it, like those patches of the winter sky seen through cloud vistas in the west before sundown. Yet a single glass of its water held up to the light is as colourless as an equal quantity of air. It is well known that a large plate of glass will have a green tint, owing, as the makers say, to its 'body', but a small piece of the same will be colorless. How large a body of Walden water would be required to reflect a green tint, I have never proved. The water of our river is black or a very dark brown to one looking directly down on it, and, like that of most ponds, imparts to the body of one bathing in it a yellowish tinge; but this water is of such crystalline purity that the body of the bather appears of an alabaster whiteness, still more unnatural, which, as the limbs are magnified and distorted withal, produces a monstrous effect, making fit studies for a Michaelangelo.

The water is so transparent that the bottom can easily be

discerned at the depth of twenty-five or thirty feet. Paddling over it, you may see many feet beneath the surface the schools of perch and shiners, perhaps only an inch long, yet the former easily distinguished by their transverse bars, and you think that they must be ascetic fish that find a subsistence there. Once, in the winter, many years ago, when I had been cutting holes through the ice in order to catch pickerel, as I stepped ashore I tossed my axe back onto the ice, but, as if some evil genius directed it, it slid four or five rods directly into one of the holes, where the water was twenty-five feet deep. Out of curiosity, I lay down on the ice and looked through the hole, until I saw the axe a little to one side, standing on its head, with its helve erect and gently swaying to and fro with the pulse of the pond; and there it might have stood erect and swaying till in the course of time the handle rotted off, if I had not disturbed it. Making another hole directly over it with an ice chisel which I had, and cutting down the longest birch which I could find in the neighborhood with my knife, I made a slip noose, which I attached to its end, and, letting it down carefully, passed it over the knob of the handle, and drew it by a line along the birch, and so pulled the axe out again.

The shore is composed of a belt of smooth rounded white stones like paving-stones, excepting one or two short sand beaches, and is so steep that in many places a single leap will carry you into water over your head; and were it not for its remarkable transparency, that would be the last seen of its bottom till it rose on the opposite side. Some think it is bottomless. It is nowhere muddy, and a casual observer would say that there were no weeds at all in it; and of noticeable plants, except in the little meadows recently over-flowed, which do not properly belong to it, a closer scrutiny does not detect a flag nor a bulrush, nor even a lily, yellow or white, but only a few small heartleaves and potamogetons, and perhaps a water target or two; all of which however a bather might not perceive; and these plants are clean and bright like the element they grow in. The stones extend a rod or two into the water, and then the bottom is pure sand, except in the deepest parts, where there is usually a little sediment, probably from the decay of the leaves which have been wafted onto it so many successive falls, and a bright green weed is brought up on anchors even in midwinter.

We have one other pond just like this, White Pond, in Nine Acre Corner, about two and a half miles westerly; but, though I am acquainted with most of the ponds within a dozen miles of this center, I do not know a third of this pure and well-like character. Successive nations perchance have drank at, admired, and fathomed it, and passed away, and still its water is green and pellucid as ever. Not an intermitting spring! Perhaps on that spring morning when Adam and Eve were driven out of Eden, Walden Pond was already in existence, and even then breaking up in a gentle spring rain accompanied with mist and a southerly wind, and covered with myriads of ducks and geese, which had not heard of the fall, when still such pure lakes sufficed them. Even then it had commenced to rise and fall, and had clarified its waters and colored them of the hue they now wear, and obtained a patent of Heaven to be the only Walden Pond in the world and distiller of celestial dews. Who knows in how many unremembered nations' literatures this has been the Castalian Fountain? or what nymphs presided over it in the Golden Age? It is a gem of the first water which Concord wears in her coronet.

Yet perchance the first who came to this well have left some trace of their footsteps. I have been surprised to detect encircling the pond, even where a thick wood has just been cut down on the shore, a narrow shelf-like path in the deep hillside, alternately rising and falling, approaching and receding from the water's edge, as old probably as the race of man here, worn by the feet of aboriginal hunters, and still from time to time unwittingly trodden by the present occupants of the land. This is particularly distinct to one standing on the middle of the pond in winter, just after a light snow has fallen, appearing as a clear undulating white line, unobscured by

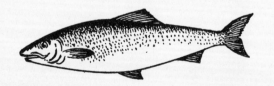

weeds and twigs, and very obvious a quarter of a mile off in many places where in summer it is hardly distinguishable close at hand. The snow reprints it, as it were, in clear white type alto-relievo. The ornamented grounds of villas which will one day be built here may still preserve some trace of this.

The pond rises and falls, but whether regularly or not, and within what period, nobody knows, though, as usual, many pretend to know. It is commonly higher in the winter and lower in the summer, though not corresponding to the general wet and dryness. I can remember when it was a foot or two lower, and also when it was at least five feet higher, than when I lived by it. There is a narrow sandbar running into it, with very deep water on one side, on which I helped boil a kettle of chowder, some six rods from the main shore, about the year 1824, which it has not been possible to do for twenty-five years; and, on the other hand, my friends used to listen with incredulity when I told them, that a few years later I was accustomed to fish from a boat in a secluded cove in the woods, fifteen rods from the only shore they knew, which place was long since converted into a meadow. This makes a difference of level, at the outside, of six or seven feet; and yet the water shed by the surrounding hills is insignificant in amount, and this overflow must be referred to causes which affect the deep springs. This same summer the pond has begun to fall again. It is remarkable that this fluctuation, whether periodical or not, appears thus to require many years for its accomplishment. I have observed one rise and a part of two falls, and I expect that a dozen or fifteen years hence the water will again be as low as I have ever known it. Flints' Pond, a mile eastward, allowing for the disturbance occasioned by its inlets and outlets, and the smaller intermediate ponds also, sympathize with Walden, and recently attained their greatest height at the same time with the latter. The same is true, as far as my observation goes, of White Pond.

The rise and fall of Walden at long intervals serves this use at least: the water standing at this great height for a year or more, though it makes it difficult to walk round it, kills the shrubs and trees which have sprung up about its edge since the last rise – pitch pines, birches, alders, aspens, and others – and, falling again, leaves an unobstructed shore; for, unlike many ponds and all waters which are subject to a daily tide, its shore is cleanest when the water is lowest. On the side of the pond next my house a row of pitch pines, fifteen feet high, has been killed and tipped over as if by a lever, and thus a stop put to their encroachments; and their size indicates how many years have elapsed since the last rise to this height. By this fluctuation the pond asserts its title to a shore, and thus the *shore* is *shorn*, and the trees cannot hold it by right possession. These are the lips of the lake on which no beard grows. It licks its chaps from time to time. When the water is at its height, the alders, willows, and maples send forth a mass of fibrous red roots several feet long from all sides of their stems in the water, and to the height of three or four feet from the ground, in the effort to maintain themselves; and I have known the high-blueberry bushes about the shore, which commonly produce no fruit, bear an abundant crop under these circumstances.

Some have been puzzled to tell how the shore became so regularly paved. My townsmen have all heard the tradition, the oldest people tell me that they heard it in their youth, that anciently the Indians were holding a powwow upon a hill here, which rose as high into the heavens as the pond now sinks deep into the earth, and they used much profanity, as the story goes, though this vice is one of which the Indians were never guilty, and while they were thus engaged the hill shook and suddenly sank, and only one old squaw, named Walden, escaped, and from her the pond was named. It has been conjectured that when the hill shook these stones rolled down its side and became the present shore. It is very certain, at any rate, that once there was no pond here, and now there is one; and this Indian fable does not in any respect conflict with the account of that ancient settler whom I have mentioned, who remembers so well when he first came here with his divining rod, saw a thin vapor rising from the sward, and the hazel pointed steadily downward, and he concluded to dig a well here. As for the stones, many still think that they are hardly to be accounted for by the action of the waves on these hills: but I

observe that the surrounding hills are remarkably full of the same
kind of stones, so that they have been obliged to pile them up in
walls on both sides of the railroad cut nearest the pond; and,
moreover, there are most stones where the shore is most abrupt; so
that, unfortunately, it is no longer a mystery to me. I detect the
paver. If the name was not derived from that of some English
locality – Saffron Walden, for instance – one might suppose that it
was called originally *Walled-in* Pond.

From the FISHING GAZETTE

(1884)

I HAVE CONTINUED MY EXPERIMENTS IN RELATION TO BRANDY AS A
means of restoring life to a dying fish, the results being, in the
main, highly satisfactory.

It was highly interesting to see the plucky manner a trout battled
with his fainting condition, after a dose of brandy, and came out
the conqueror.

Strange to say, the salmon did not once attempt to rouse
himself after being dosed, the consequence being fatal to him. This
was the only fish that succumbed under the treatment.

As regards the dace, I had him out of the water three times of
five minutes each. He was exceedingly faint and almost dead, but
immediately the brandy was given he pulled himself together and
in the course of a few minutes not only recovered, but darted
around with a rapidity positively amazing.

From FLY-RODS AND FLY-TACKLE

BY HENRY P. WELLS (1885)

SOME FISHERMEN THINK THAT ANY ROD THEY BUY AND PAY FOR should stand any form of abuse, and if it does not, the rod-maker is blamed and his work decried. The makers know this, and that their reputation for skilled and honest work is as sensitive as that of a woman . . . To such of my readers as wish to buy and do not care to make, I would say that the maker who has a reputation, will do his best to maintain it. If he once turned out good work, competition will force him to do so still. If he has the skill, you may be sure that he will use it. No one knows better than he that one bad rod will do him more harm than a hundred first class in every respect will benefit him . . .

From DAYS AND NIGHTS OF SALMON FISHING

BY WILLIAM SCROPE (1843)

William Scrope (1772–1852) only wrote two books in his lifetime, the *Art of Deer Stalking* and *Days and Nights of Salmon Fishing*. He didn't have to work for a living and so he divided his time between a number of pursuits such as painting, travelling, field sports as well as angling. He was a friend of Sir Walter Scott, who much admired his artistic skills, and who puts in a rather curmudgeonly appearance in the following extract in which Scrope describes the art of 'leistering' – fishing with a spear – on the river Tweed in the Borders of Scotland. As John Ashley-Cooper, one of the great salmon fisherman of the twentieth century, once said, 'The Tweed has provided inspiration for a wealth of books; but none of them is more outstanding than that masterpiece *Days and Nights of Salmon Fishing* by William Scrope . . . No keen Tweed angler should fail to study this book.'

* * *

THE BOAT IN GENERAL USE FOR BURNING AT NIGHT IS LARGER THAN the rod-fishing boats, as more room and steadiness is required. In the centre of it, close to the side of which the 'leisterers' strike the fish, is a pole fixed vertically with a frame on top of it formed of ribs to contain combustibles.

Three men were sufficient to man the boat; one at the head, another at the stern, as boatman and leisterers, and the third at the centre to kill the fish and trim the fire. But it will contain more men if necessary.

The remainder of the day having been spent in making arrangements, and the proper hour now being come, Harry Otter and Charlie Purdie went out from the pavilion to meet the party, who were to assemble at eight o'clock about a mile and a half up the river. The night was most favourable, it being utterly dark, and not a sough of air stirring. With caution and difficulty they felt their way step by step at the rocky base of the Scaur, where it dips into the river, till they descried the boat which was to take them across it at the Brig-end Pool. The clanking of the chains as it was loosened and flung on the planks sounded harshly in the silence of night; the oars dipped duly, and they were soon on the opposite side of the river, by which means they cut off a great sweep of the haugh, 'a huge half-moon, a monstrous cantle out,' and proceeded in a more direct line to their mark. They went on in darkness through the chilly dews, now and then stumbling into patches of furze which were scattered over the haugh; soon they begin to hear the rushing of the waters through the gorge of Carrywheel; now it breaks full and loud upon the ear, for they are arrived at the base of the wooden brae that overhangs the cast.

Two groups of men, but dimly seen, here await their arrival; one consisting of spectators lying on the ground with their plaids thrown athwart their bodies, and the other of the heroes who were to figure in the grand operation, these latter were sitting on the boats, and on the masses of rock beside them at the water edge.

All being now ready, a light was struck; and the spark being applied to rags steeped in pitch, and to fragments of tar barrels, they blazed up at once amidst the gloom, like the sudden flash from the crater of a volcano. The ruddy light glared on the rough features and dark dresses of the leisterers in cutting flames directly met by black shadows – an effect which those will best understand who in the Eternal City have seen the statues in the Vatican by torchlight. Extending itself, it reddened the shelving rocks above, and glanced upon the blasted arms of trees, slowly perishing in their struggle for existence amongst the stony crevices; it glowed upon the hanging wood, on fir, birch, broom, and bracken, half-veiled, or half-revealed, as they were more or less prominent. The form of things remote from the concentrated light was dark and dubious; even the trees on the summit of the brae sank into obscurity.

The principals now sprang into the boats. Harry Otter stood at the head, and Charlie Purdie at the stern. These men regulated the course of the craft with their leisters; the auxiliaries were stationed between them, and the light was in the centre by the boat side. The logs, steeped as they were in pitch, crackled and burned fiercely, sending up a column of black smoke. As the rude forms of the men rose up in their dark attire, wielding their long leisters, with the streaks of light that glared partially upon them, and surrounded as they were by the shades of night, you might almost have fancied yourself in the realms below, with Pluto and his grim associates, embarked on a Stygian lake.

But as the sports began and as the Scotch accent prevailed, the illusion passed away, for no poet that I am aware of has made the swarthy and mysterious personages express themselves in the language of Tweedside; nor could one fancy salmon in the Styx, though they might well disport in the streams of the happy fields beyond.

'Now, my lads,' says the master, 'take your places. Tom, you stand next to me. Sandy, go on the other side of Tom, and do you, Jamie, keep in the middle, and take tent to cap the boats well over

the rapids. Rob, do you and Tom Purdie keep good lights and fell
the fish. Hallo, Tom, you have smuggled a leister into the boat for
your own use!'

'Aye, aye, that have I, joust for mine ain deversion, ye ken.'

'Well, well, you may just keep it, for you are a stout chiel, and
it would be hard work to get it from you, besides, no one can use it
more dexterously than yourself. Now then, we will push the boat
up the cheek of the stream till we come to the head of it. That will
do. Now shoot her across the gorge, and down she goes merrily,
broadside foremost according to rule. Cap, Charlie, cap, man. We
are drifting down like mad; keep back your end of the boat.'

'Awheel, awheel, she gangs cannily noo, look, uncle, a muckle
fish before ye or ever ye kent, the maister's leister gaed through
him, and played all dife. That side, that side, Jamie – he's rinnin up
to get past. Od ye have him and I hae anither, and anither. Keep a
gude light, Tom. Now let us take up the boat to the head of the
stream, or ever we look the stanes, for there war a muckle fush
gaed by that nane o ye gomrells ever saw. There, we are nigh
enough now haud your hand, and let her faw doon again; hey, but I
see him the noo afore me – ou, what an awful beast!'

So saying, Charlie drove his leister furiously at him, but
whether one of the prongs struck against the edge of the rock
above him, which prevented its descent to the bottom or whatever
other cause, the stroke was unsuccessful, and as he lifted the barren
weapon out of the water, there arose a merry shout and guffaw
from the spectators on the shore.

'Cap, cap,' cried Charlie, 'now hand yer hand, gie me up the boat
– od, but I'll hae him yet, he's gane amangst thae hiding stanes.'

So saying, Charlie brought the head of the boat to the stream,
pushed her higher up, and pulled her ashore; he then landed, and
seizing a brand out of the fire, put it into Jamieson's hand, who
preceded his eager steps like a male Thais, or one of the Eumenides
in pantaloons. He now stood upon a rock which hung over the
river, and from that eminence, and with the assistance of the
firebrand examined the bottom of it very carefully. His body was
bent over the water, and his ready leister held almost vertically as

the light glared on his face you might see the keen, glistening eye. In an instant he raised up his leister, and down he sprang from the rock right into the river, and with wild bound nailed the salmon to the channel. There was a struggle with his arms for a few seconds; he then passed his hands down the pole of the weapon a little way, brought himself vertically over the fish, and lifted him aloft, cheered by shouts from his friends on the shore.

Two or three more fish were taken amongst the stones at the tail of the cast, and the sport in the Carrywheel now being ended the fish were stowed in the hold of the boat, the crew jumped ashore, and a right hearty appeal was made to the whisky bottle.

It was first tendered to the veteran Tom Purdie, to whom it was always observed to have natural gravitation, but to the astonishment of all, he barely put his lips to the quaigh, and passed it to his nephew.

'Why, uncle mon, what the deil's come owre ye? I niver kent ye refuse a drappie afore, no, not sin I war a callant, I canno thole to see ye gang that gait.'

'Why, I'll tell ye what it is, Charlie. I got a repreef from Sir Walter for being fou the ither nicht.'

'Eh, uncle, how was that?'

'"Why," said Sir Walter, "Tom," he says, "I sent for ye on Monday, and ye were not at hame at aight o'clock. I doubt ye were fou, Tom." "I'll just tell ye the hale truth," says I. "I gaied roond by the men at wark at Rymers Glen, and cam in by Tarfield, then I went to Darnick, and had a glass wi Sandy Trummel at Susy, and I war joust coming awa when Rob steppit in, and cried for half a mutchkin. I wasna for takking mair, but the glasses were filled, and I did not like be bat wi them, so I tuk mine." "And is that all ye had, Tom?" said Sir Walter. "Aye, indeed it was," said I, "but Heaven have a care o' me, I never was the war of it till I was ganging up by Jemmy Mercer's by Coats Green and when I cam up by Kerr side I wanted to see Maister Laidlaw, but I thocht I dirstna gang in and how I got hame I dinna ken for I niver minded it nae mair, but our wife in a terrible bad key the morning, because I was sair wanted last nicht."

' "Well," said the maister, "you mun never do the like again, Tom." We then ganged into the wood, and thinned the trees and I laboured with the axe at thae Sir Walter marked.

' "No, Tom," says he, "you will go hame with me, for you have been working very hard, and a glass of whisky will do you good"; and he cawwed to Nicholson to bring Tom a glass o' Glenlivet. I tuk it doon, and mon, if yed found it – it beat a' the whisky I ever tasted in my life. "Well, Tom," says Sir Walter, "how do you feel after it? Do ye think another glass will do ye ony harm?" I said naethin, but I thocht I would like anither, and Nicholson poured out ain, and I tuk it. Then the maister said: "Tom, do ye feel any the war for it?" "Na, na," said I, "but it's terrible powerful and three times as strang as ony whusky I ever drank in my life." "Then, Tom," says Sir Walter, "never tell me that three glasses o' Sussy's whusky will fill ye fou, when ye have drank twa o' mine, which you say is three times as strong, an' you feel a' the better for it."

'Hey, mon, I was niver so ta'en by the face in a' my life! I didna ken where to luk. The deil faw me if ever he cotcht me so again!'

Tom Purdie's forbearance, however, was not of an enduring quality; his eyes glistened as he followed the course of the bottle; three times was his arm extended to make a grab at it, and thrice did he draw it back with modest confusion. At length when all were served he could hold out no longer, but elongating his dexter, he laid fast the bottle, and filling the quaigh to the brim, 'Here goes,' said he, 'to the lousy stranger.' After he had drunk, and mended his draught, he kept the bottle in his own custody with a pretty smart allowance in it, in character for residuary legatee. I had an account, however, to settle with him; for being the only stranger in the company, I fancied his toast meant a reflection on my cleanliness. What did he mean by the dirty and degrading epithet? This I demanded, advancing with a war-like countenance and leister at rest; and had not Tom been in a very benign humour this book might never have been inflicted on the public, for the man was well armed and resolute, and might have leistered me according to his art. But putting on his sweetest smile, he assured me that by the 'lousy stranger' he meant a newly run fish, with the tide lice on it, 'which,' said he, 'is far the best ye ken.' This I well knew, though the application did not occur to me at the moment. And here, by the way, I beg to observe that you may know the best clean fish by their having tide lice on them.

* * *

'COME, COME, LADS,' SAYS THE MASTER, 'HOLD YOUR CLISH-MA-clavers, for we are just going into Brig-end Pool; so keep back the boat as well as you can, or we shall go fiery fast over the stream.'

As the boat neared the pool, the men shouted: 'Auld Michael! Auld Michael! the charm for auld Michael Scott; trim the boat, and take care the muckle wizard doesna loup intill her.'

'Od lads!' cries Tom Purdie, 'pit yer best fut foremost; they are lying afore us like sacks, and will be as thick as you can dab them up. Mind the licht, Sandy, and take care that kipper doesna wallop out of the boat. See what a muckle fush Charlie has got!'

In fact the men were making great slaughter, and when we had gone over the pool two or three times, had half-filled the boat with spoil, so as they found they were well laden, they called to Rob Colyard to come forward with his cart to take them home.

'Shove the boat to the shore; Colyard come forrard wi' the cart; that do, mon, aw hond to wark; count the fush as ye put them in, Charlie, how mony hae ye counted?'

'There jest be a hunder and twa, great and sma' – whitling, bull trout, sammots, and a' thegither!'

* * *

WE NOW MARCHED HOME WITH OUR SPOIL TRIUMPHANT – Sandy in front, with a blazing beacon over his shoulder to light our steps, as has been practised from time immemorial; the others with the fish and leisters. One of the spectators began a *concordia discors* with his bagpipes, but bade us adieu at Melrose

Bridge and the dulcet sounds died away among the pine woods and
furze brakes of the Eildon Hills.

THE TAKING OF A SALMON

BY THOMAS TOD STODDART (1866)

Thomas Tod Stoddart (1810–80) gained a reputation as a fine
fisherman and author. As well as a number of books on fishing, he
wrote an autobiography, published the year after his death. There is
a happy and lively jauntiness about his verse which invites the
reader to join him in a fishing expedition.

* * *

I   A birr! a whirr! a salmon's on,
        A goodly fish, a thumper!
        Bring up, bring up the ready gaff,
        And when we land him we shall quaff
        Another glorious bumper!
        Hark! 'tis the music of the reel,
        The strong, the quick, the steady:
        The line darts from the circling wheel,
        Have all things right and ready.

II   A birr! a whirr! the salmon's out
        Far on the rushing river,
        He storms the stream with edge of might,
        And like a brandish'd sword of light,
        Rolls flashing oe'r the surges white,
        A desperate endeavour!
        Hark to the music of the reel!
        The fitful and the grating;
        It pants along the breathless wheel,
        Now hurried, now abating.

III   A birr! a whirr! the salmon's off!
        No, no, we still have got him;
        The wily fish has sullen grown,
        And, like a bright embedded stone,
        Lies gleaming at the bottom.
        Hark to the music of the reel!
        'Tis hush'd, it hath forsaken;
        With care we'll guard the slumbering wheel
        Until its notes awaken.

IV   A birr! a whirr! the salmon's up!
        Give line, give line and measure;
        And now he turns, keep down a-head
        And lead him as a child is led,
        And land him at your leisure.
        Hark to the music of the reel!
        'Tis welcome, it is glorious;
        It wanders round the exultant wheel,
        Returning and victorious.

V   A birr! a whirr! the salmon's in,
        Upon the bank extended;
        The princely fish lies gasping slow,
        His brilliant colours come and go,
        Silver alternating with snow,
        All beautifully blended.
        Hark to the music of the reel!
        It murmurs and it closes;
        Silence falls on the conquering wheel,
        The wearied line reposes.

VI   No birr! no whirr! the salmon's ours:
        The noble fish, the thumper!
        Strike through his gill the ready gaff,
        And bending homewards we shall quaff
        The overflowing bumper!

Hark to the music of the reel!
We listen with devotion;
There's something in that circling wheel
That stirs the heart's emotion!

A COLD BATH

BY A. NELSON CHENEY (1878)

April 1st, 1878 – Opening day. Fished Halfway brook from Morgan brook to, and through, the woods; then fished Ogden brook from Van Husen's road to Gleason's. Banks more than full of roily snow water; weather decidedly cold; strong wind from the Northwest; cloudy sky. Caught one small trout that I returned to his native element to grow; discovered from my single specimen of the *Salvelinus fontinalis* that they have the same bright spots that they have always had; look the same, smell the same, *feel* the same; other peculiarities lacking. Warm sun and rain required to develop the characteristics we so much admire in our leaping friend. Managed to fall in the Ogden brook – in fact went in without the slightest difficulty, amid applause from the bank; discovered from my involuntary plunge that the water is just as wet as last year, and if memory serves, a trifle colder. Reached home in the evening, cold, wet, tired and hungry. Nevertheless, had a most *glorious* time.

From My Fishing Days and Fishing Ways

by J.W. Martin (1906)

It was a typical Christmas morning of the good old-fashioned sort; a slight misty haze, aided by frost, had clothed the trees and hedges in a fantastic garb of glittering, scintillating white. Scarcely a breath of wind was blowing, but what there was brought with it in the face of the early morning sportsman a taste of the coldness of the north. The sun was just rising above the spur of a range of low hills that flanked the south-eastern horizon, and gleamed with a dull misty red, throwing a series of strange lights and shadows across its track, and lighting up in a brilliant silvery sheen the tops of the distant trees. Underfoot the grass crunched with every step, and all along the river's edge, and clinging lovingly to the lowest twigs of the overhanging scattered bushes, was a thin skim of ice, that swayed and dipped with every swirl of the current.

It most certainly was not a morning for a butterfly fisherman to be out, whose idea of fishing was green trees and leaves, to be lulled into sleep by a lazy drone from a thousand insects, under a cloudless sun. I was a bit younger and more hardy on the day that I have in my mind's eye just now, and rather gloried in the beauties of a keen winter's morn, and considered a day's chubbing under the conditions of that day the very beau-ideal of a sportsman's life; for be it known to all and sundry that our leather-mouthed friend the chub is the sporting fish *par excellence* of a keen and frosty day, pike and grayling not excepted, by me at any rate.

I had left the people of the house that Christmas morn – the women folk, at any rate – a clear field and no favour to prepare the turkey, the plum-pudding, and the various indigestible items that go to make up that time-honoured meal known as the Christmas dinner. Strict orders and sundry injunctions had been given as to the time to return, and an hour later I stood in the valley of the grand old river Trent, watching the wintry sun climbing slowly up the distant hill, and lighting up the whole landscape in a glorious halo of dancing white. The river flowed along, curling under the roots of those old bushes, ever and anon swirling with a gurgling splash as an eddy was sucked underneath the hollow clay bank, then swirled out again until finally lost under the dark shadows of a distant bough. It was extremely inviting, in spite of its somewhat wintry aspect. The water was just tinged with a very faint colour: a stone on the bottom could be detected about two feet down.

Chub are fish that can be found in a suitable place during very cold and frosty weather, even when the place is not more than three or four feet deep. It is a mistake to think that chub can only be found in very deep water during the cold weather; I have found them at all depths, when the float had to be fourteen feet away from the hook, and when it was only two feet away. This particular part of the river, under the boughs and overhanging banks, varied from two to five feet in depth, and contained some pretty fair fish, as previous visits and experiences had more than once clearly proved, and I looked forward to an enjoyable, not to say exciting time.

If there is one bait more than another that I swear by for the fish now under notice, when weather is cold and frosty, that bait is bullock's pith, raw, for the hook, and bullock's brains, boiled hard and finely minced, for ground-bait, if that particular operation can be called ground-baiting. It was rather a difficult job, getting that bait on Christmas Eve, but by great good luck a butcher friend obliged me with a set. The brains were well washed and cleaned, all the blood and impurities being carefully removed; they were then tied up in a square of calico and boiled for nearly an hour, until they became tough and hard.

The pith itself, which I suppose I need not say is the spinal cord of the beast, was skinned, divided into short ropes as it were, and well washed and cleaned. This is all that is required; the inner fine skin is useful for holding the bait more firmly on the hook, the course, rough outside skin only being removed.

It was a morning made for chub fishing – water in the very best condition, and a stream running that was strong enough to carry the float and tackle onward without check or hindrance. This combination of affair suggested an enjoyable time, and something to show for it at the end. The first place I tried was along the front of a low overhanging bank, crowned with a couple of bushes whose lowest boughs touched the water some four feet out in the stream: water about the same number of feet deep.

Taking out the shell and scissors, I put a bit of the boiled brains about the size of a large walnut in the former and clipped it up as small as ever I could, then putting sufficient water in the shell to cover the brains, well stirred and mixed them together, finally throwing the contents of the shell a few yards higher up stream, so that it would reach mid-water or a little deeper by the time it got to the bushes, taking care that it sank a foot or so in front of the boughs and whirled about the stream in tiny fragments. If you are careful where you throw the clipped-up brains and mix and stir well in a little water, they will sink attractively, exactly where you want them.

My pith was in short ropes about six or eight inches long, and say half an inch thick. Clipping a bit off about three quarters of an inch long, I inserted the hook two or three times, until the bait was worked up the shank, and no more long ends hanging loose below the bend than could possibly be helped.

Then I stood well up above the stream, gently tossing out the tackle so that the float would travel some foot or eighteen inches in front of the boughs, with the bait about six inches above the bottom (hitting that distance nicely), taking care that the float did not travel quite so fast as it would have liked to do. This gentle holding back of the float causes the bait to travel a little in advance, and the strike, when a fish takes it, is more sharp and direct. Now this is most important in any sort of stream-fishing, when the float must of necessity be a good distance below where you stand: the bait must not trail behind the float.

Steadily onward went that float, three quarters of an inch of its red tip showing above the water, until it reached about the centre of the first bush, when it shot suddenly downwards with that sideways glide so characteristic of a chub bite when he means business. An instantaneous response from the rod-point resulted in a heavy plunge and a tackle as fast as a thief in a mill, which no amount of sawing this way and that could loosen. I have heard my old friend, the late Tom Sunman, say that a chub hardly ever takes bait the first time it goes past him; he simply looks out for a convenient stump or root, and next time, seizing the bait, dashes headlong round its chosen retreat.

Anyhow, there it was, a bad start; the first swim down had resulted in a lost fish and a broken tackle. Luckily the hook itself only had gone, so it was very easy to repair the damages.

The swim being hopelessly disturbed for the time being, I went on to a nice little eddy that curled inside a hollow shelving bank. Repeating the operation that had led to such a disastrous result before, the bag speedily had its first occupant. Ten more minutes' careful trail there failed to add a companion to its lonely condition. The three next swims and more than half an hour's work also failed to produce any results whatever, and I began to think that after all the bag would be extremely light.

A little lower down stream, at the corner of a small spinney, was a short length of old decaying camp-shedding, with one or two rather dangerous fasteners projecting from it. This swim was a little deeper than the usual run just there, and it looked so tempting that I determined to give it a little extra ground-bait and a more extended trail, in spite of the fine skins of ice that encrusted every rotten timber and threatened to cut asunder the line if the fish bolted for that particular bit of cover. I got here the best brace of the day, both well over three pounds, and had two rather bad smashes among these villainous piles, stones, sunken timber, and old iron bolts.

About fifty yards lower down stream the bank suddenly rose to a height of nine or ten feet; a heavy flood some time or other had there swept out a little sheltered bay, into which the stream raced with considerable force, forming a beautiful umbrella-like eddy that curled and dimpled round and round, edging a mass of yeast-like foam six inches up the steep bank on the opposite corner. This swim was about three feet deep, and always worth trying. But now a two-pounder only rewarded my very best efforts.

A distant village clock, through the clear winter atmosphere, now chimed out the hour, and reminded me that our Christmas fishing trip was rapidly drawing to a close, and that it would soon be time to pack up and away. There was just time to try the bushes where four hours earlier I had had my first mishap; so I retraced my steps, passing the succession of curling eddies, dipping boughs, old wooden camp-shedding, and rattling streams that had afforded me such delight during the short hours of that winter's day. This time I managed, by exercising a quick and sudden pressure, to land the brother chub to the one hooked and lost in the morning.

The rooks were homing slowly overhead, a cloud of pigeons were whirling up the slope of a distant wooden hill, and a flock of green plovers were alternately showing their black and white as they turned from side to side during their flight across the meadow on the opposite bank, when I turned away for the hour's homeward march that lay between me and that Christmas dinner, for which the day and its results had given me such an appetite. The bag contained six chub weighing close on fifteen pounds – the largest nearly three and a half pounds, the smallest just under two pounds.

THE FAIRY-LIKE FLY

BY JAMES A. HENSHALL, MD (1855)

Fly-fishers are usually brain-workers in society. Along the banks of purling streams, beneath the shadows of umbrageous trees, or in the secluded nooks of charming lakes, they have ever been found, drinking deep of the invigorating forces of nature – giving rest and tone to over-taxed brains and wearied nerves – while gracefully wielding the supple rod, the invisible leader, and the fairy-like fly.

From CHENEYS AND THE HOUSE OF RUSSELL

BY J.A. FROUDE (1879)

James Anthony Froude (1818–94) was educated at Westminster and later at Oriel College, Oxford. During his lifetime he wrote a great many books, amongst them his *History of England from the Fall of Wolsey to the Defeat of the Spanish Armada*, *The English in Ireland in the Eighteenth Century* and *The English in the West Indies*. *Cheneys and the House of Russell* was published in 1879. It captures the real essence of the English countryside and the leisurely pursuit of the gentleman . . .

* * *

THE SUN WAS SHINING AN HOUR AGO. IT IS NOW RAINING; IT RAINED all yesterday; the clouds are coming up from the south and the wind is soft as oil. The day is still before us, and it is a day made for trout fishing . . .

No river in England holds finer trout, nor trout more willing to be caught. A day's fishing at Cheneys means a day by the best water in England in the fisherman's paradise of solitude.

The water-keeper is at the window – best of keepers – for he will accept a sandwich perhaps for luncheon, a pull from your flask, and a cigar out of your case, but other fee on no condition. The rain he tells me has raised the water, and the large fish are on the move, the May-fly has been down for two days. They were feeding on it last evening. If the sky clears they will take well in the afternoon; but the fly will not show till the rain stops.

Breakfast over, I start for the lower water. I have my boy with me home for the holidays. He carries the landing net, and we splash through the rain to the mill . . .

The small fish take freely – some go back into the water, the few in good condition into the basket, which, after a field or two becomes perceptibly heavier. The governor, a small humble bee, used to be a good fly at Cheneys, and so did the black alder. Neither of them is of any use to-day. The season has been cold and late. The March brown answers best, with the never-failing red spinner. After running rapidly through two or three meadows, the river opens into a broad smooth shallow, where the trout are larger, and the water being extremely clear, are specially difficult to catch. In such a place as this, it is useless to throw your fly at random upon the stream. You must watch for a fish which is rising, and you must fish for him till you either catch him or disturb him. It is not enough to go below him and throw upwards, for though he lies with his head up-stream, his projecting eye looks back over his shoulders. You must hide behind a bunch of rushes. You must crawl along the grass with arm only raised. If the sun is shining and the shadow of your rod glances over the gravel, you may get up and walk away. No fish within sight will stir then to the daintiest cast.

I see a fish close to the bank on the opposite side, lazily lifting his head as a fly floats past him. It is a long throw, but the wind is fair, and he is worth an effort – once, twice, three times I fail to reach to him. The fourth I land the fly on the far bank, and draw it gently off upon his very nose. He swirls in the water like a salmon as he sweeps round to seize it. There is a splash – a sharp jerk, telling unmistakably that something has given way. Large fish may break you honestly in weeds or round a rock or stump, and only fate is to blame, but to let yourself be broken on the first strike is unpardonable. What can have happened? Alas, the red spinner has snapped in two at the bend – a new fly bought last week at ____'s, whose boast it has been that no fly of his was ever known to break or bend.

One grumbles on these occasions, for it is always the best fish which one loses; and as imagination is free, one may call him what weight one pleases. The damage is soon repaired. The basket fills

fast as trout follows trout. It still rains, and I begin to think that I
have had enough of it. I have promised to be at the mill midday,
and then we shall see.

Evidently the sky means mischief. Black thunder-clouds pile up
to windward, and heavy drops continue falling. But there is a break
in the south as I walk back by the bank – a gleam of sunshine spans
the valley with a rainbow, and an actual May-fly or two sails by
which I see greedily swallowed. The keeper is waiting; he looks
scornfully into my basket. Fish – did I call these herrings fish? I must
try the upper water at all events. The large trout were feeding, but
the fly was not yet properly on – we can have our luncheon first.

How pleasant is luncheon on mountain side or river's bank,
when you fling yourself down on fern or heather after your
morning's work, and no daintiest *entrée* had ever such flavour as
your sandwiches, and no champagne was ever so exquisite as the
fresh stream water just tempered from your whisky flask. Then
follows the smoke, when the keeper fills his pipe at your bag, and old
adventures are talked over, and the conversation wanders on through
anecdotes and experiences, till, as you listen to the shrewd sense and
kindly feeling of your companion, you become aware that the steep
difference which you had imagined to be created by education and
habits of life had no existence save in your own conceit. Fortune is
less unjust than she seems, and true hearts and clear-judging healthy
minds, are bred as easily in the cottage as the palace . . .

Below the shallow there is a pool made by a small weir, over
which the flood is now rushing – on one side there is an open
hatchway, with the stream pouring through. The banks are bushy,
and over the deepest part of the pool the stem of a large ash
projects into the river. Yesterday, when the water was lower, the
keeper saw a four-pounder lying under that stem. Between the weir
and the trees it is an awkward spot, but difficulty is the charm of
fly-fishing. The dangerous drop fly must be taken off; a drop fly is
only fit for open water, where there is neither weed nor stump. The
March brown is sent skimming at the tail of the casting line, to be
dropped, if possible, just above the ash, and to be carried under it
by the stream. It has been caught in a root, so it seems; or it is foul

somewhere. Surely no fish ever gave so dead a pull. No; it is no root. The line shoots under the bank. There is a broad flash of white just below the surface, a moment's struggle, the rod springs straight, and the line comes back unbroken. The March brown is still floating at the end of it. It was a big fish, perhaps the keeper's very big one; he must have been lightly hooked, and have rubbed the fly out of his mouth.

But let us look closer. The red spinner had played false in the morning; may not something like it have befallen the March brown? Something like it, indeed. The hook has straightened out as if, instead of steel, it had been made of copper. A pretty business! I try another, and another, with the same result. The heavy trout take them, one bends and the next breaks. Oh!___ ___! Well for Charles Kingsley that he was gone before he heard of a treason which would have broken his trust in man. You in whose praise I have heard him so often eloquent! You never dealt in shoddy goods. You were faithful if all else were faithless, and redeemed the credit of English tradesmen. You had not then been in the school of progress and learnt that it was the buyer's business to distinguish good from bad. You never furnished your customers with cheap and nasty wares, fair looking to the eye and worthless to the touch and trial. In those days you dealt with gentlemen, and you felt and traded like a gentleman yourself. And now you, too, have gone the way of your fellows. You are making a fortune as you call it, out of the reputation which you won honourably in better days. You have given yourself over to competition and semblance. You have entered for the race among the sharpers, and will win by knavery and tricks like the rest. I will not name you for the sake of old times, when C.K. and I could send you a description of a fly from the furthest corner of Ireland, and by return post would come a packet tied on hooks which Kendal and Limerick might equal, but could not excel. You may live on undenounced for me; but read C.K.'s books over again; repent of your sins, go back to honest ways, and renounce the new gospel in which whosoever believes shall not be saved.

But what is to be done? Spite of the rain the river is now

covered with drowned May-flies, and the trout are taking them all round. I have new May-flies from the same quarter in my book, but it will be more vexation to try them. Luckily for me there are a few old ones surviving from other days. The gut is brown with age – but I must venture it. If this breaks I will go home, lock away my rod, and write an essay on the effects of the substitution of Political Economy for the Christian faith.

On then goes one of these old flies. It looks well. It bears mild strain, and, like Don Quixote with his helmet, I will not put it to a severe trial. Out it shoots over the pool, so natural looking that I cannot distinguish it from a real fly which floats at its side. I cannot, nor can that large trout in the smooth water above the fall. He takes it, springs into the air, and then darts at the weir to throw himself over. If he goes down he is lost. Hold on. He has the stream to help him, and not an inch of line can be spared. The rod bends double, but the old gut is true. Down the fall he is not to go. He turns up the pool, he makes a dart for the hatchway, – but if you can stand a trout's first rush you need not fear him in fair water afterwards. A few more efforts and he is in the net and on the bank, not the keeper's four-pounder, but a handsome fish, which I know that he will approve.

He had walked down the bank pensively while I was in the difficulty with my flies, meditating, perhaps, on idle gentlemen, and reflecting that if the tradesmen were knaves the gentlemen were correspondingly fools. He was standing by the side of the rapid stream at the head of the mill pool. It was as he had foretold; the great fish had come up, and were rolling like salmon on the top of the water gulping down the May-flies. Even when they are thus carelessly ravenous, the clearness of the river creates a certain difficulty in catching them in ordinary times, but to-day the flood made caution superfluous. They were splashing on the surface close to our feet, rolling about in a negligent gluttony which seemed to take from them every thought of danger, for a distance of at least three hundred yards.

There was no longer any alarm for the tackle, and it was but to throw the fly upon the river, near or far, for a trout instantly to seize it. There was no shy rising where suspicion balks the appetite. The fish were swallowing with a deliberate seriousness every fly which drifted within their reach, snapping their jaws upon it with a gulp of satisfaction. The only difficulty was in playing them when hooked with a delicate chalk-stream casting line. For an hour and a half it lasted, such an hour and a half of trout fishing as I had never seen and shall never see again. The ease of success at last became wearisome. Two large baskets were filled to the brim. Accident had thrown in my way a singular opportunity which it would have been wrong to abuse, so I decided to stop. We emptied out our spoils upon the grass, and the old keeper said that long as he had known the river he had never but once seen so many fish of so large size, taken in the Ches in a single day by a single rod.

The storm has passed away, the dripping trees are sparkling in the warm and watery sunset. Back then to our inn, where dinner waits us, the choicest of our own trout, pink as salmon, with the milky curd in them, and no sauce to spoil the delicacy of their flavour. Then bed, with its lavender-scented sheets and white curtains, and sleep, sound sweet sleep, that loves the country village and comes not near a London bedroom. In the morning, adieu to Cheneys, with its red gable ends and chimneys, its venerable trees, its old-world manners, and the solemn memories of its mausoleum. Adieu, too, to the river, which, 'though men may come and men may go,' has flowed and will flow on for ever, winding among its reed beds, murmuring over its gravelly fords, heedless of royal dynasties, uncaring whether Cheney or Russell calls himself lord of its waters, graciously turning the pleasant corn mills in its course, unpolluted by the fetid refuse of manufacturers, and travelling on to the ocean bright and pure and uncharged with poison, as in the old times when the priest sung mass in the church upon the hill and the sweet soft matins bell woke the hamlet to its morning prayers.

From THE SECRETS OF ANGLING

BY A.S. MOFFAT (1865)

FOR MY PART, DURING THE SUMMER SEASON, WHEN THE WATERS are warm, I am in the constant habit of wading without any protection whatever, and I never feel the slightest inconvenience from it; but I will by no means take upon me to say that everybody could do it with the same impunity, as it is a well-known fact that many people of weakly constitution have entailed upon themselves a life of misery from rheumatism and other diseases, by indiscreetly exposing their legs and feet to wet. And, as the safer practice, it will be better for the angler to avoid, if possible, both wet legs and all waterproof contrivances whatever, and content himself with enjoying his sport as best he can, 'from mossy bank or pebbly shore'. And though his creel may not exhibit so many trophies of his skill, he will at least be free from the disagreeable prospect of being condemned to swallow bushels of Blair's pills, endure the perpetual scalding of mustard-plasters, and the necessity for calling in the aid of a Bath-chair for the remainder of his life.

From CHALK-STREAM STUDIES

BY CHARLES KINGSLEY (1859)

Charles Kingsley (1819–75) is perhaps best known for his book *The Water Babies* (1863). It was written for his son, Grenville, and quickly became established as a children's classic. Kingsley spent most of his life in Hampshire where *Chalk-Stream Studies* was written; however far from confining himself to chalk streams, Kingsley also fished, amongst other places, on the Thames, the Wey and the Test, and so brings a great deal of experience to his writing.

* * *

COME, THEN, YOU WHO WANT PLEASANT FISHING DAYS. COME TO pleasant country inns, where you can always get a good dinner; or, better still, to pleasant country houses, where you can always get good society; to rivers which will always fish, brimfull in the longest droughts of summer, instead of being, as those mountain ones are, very like a turnpike-road for three weeks, and then like bottled porter for three days; to streams on which you have strong south-west breezes for a week together on a clear fishing water, instead of having, as on those mountain ones, foul rain 'spate' as long as the wind is south-west, and clearing water when the wind chops up to the north, and the chill blast of 'Clarus Aquilo' sends all the fish shivering to the bottom; streams, in a word, where you may kill fish (and large ones) four days out of five from April to October, instead of having, as you will most probably in the mountain, just one day's sport in the whole of your month's holiday. Deluded friend, who suffered in Scotland last year a month of Tantalus his torments, furnished by art and nature with rods, flies, whisky, scenery, keepers, salmon innumerable, and all that man can want, except water to fish in, and who returned, having hooked accidentally by the tail one salmon – which broke all and went to sea – why did you not stay at home and take your two-pounders and three-pounders out of the quiet chalk brook which never sank an inch through all that drought, so deep in the caverns of the hills are hidden its mysterious wells? Truly, wise men bide at home, with George Riddler, while 'a fool's eyes are in the ends of the earth'.

Repent, then; and come with me, at least in fancy, at six o'clock upon some breezy morning in the end of June, not by roaring railway nor by smoking steamer, but in the cosy four-wheel, along brown heather moors, down into green clay woodlands, over white chalk downs, past Roman camps and scattered blocks of Sarsden stone, till we descend into the long green vale where, among groves of poplar and abele, winds silver-white Whit. Come and breakfast at the neat white inn, of yore a posting-house of fame. The stables are now turned into cottages; and instead of a dozen spruce ostlers and helpers, the last of the post-boys totters sadly about the yard and looks up eagerly at the rare sight of a horse to feed. But the house keeps up enough of its ancient virtue to give us a breakfast worthy of Pantagruel's self; and after it, while we are looking out our flies, you can go and chat with the old post-boy, and hear his tales, told with a sort of chivalrous pride, of the noble lords and fair ladies before whom he has ridden in the good old times gone by – even, so he darkly hints, before 'His Royal Highness the Prince' himself. Poor old fellow, he recollects not, and he need not recollect, that these great posting houses were centres of corruption, from whence the newest vices of the metropolis were poured into the too-willing ears of village lads and lasses, and that not even the New Poor-Law itself has done more for the morality of the South of England than the substitution of the rail for coaches.

Now we will take a walk down through meadows some half mile,

> While all the land in flowery squares
> Beneath a broad and equal-blowing wind
> Smells of the coming summer,

to a scene which, as we may find its antitype anywhere for miles round, we may boldly invent for ourselves.

A red brick mill (not new red brick, of course) shall hum for ever below giant poplar-spires, which bend and shiver in the steady breeze. On its lawn laburnums shall feather down like 'dropping wells of fire', and from under them the stream shall hurry leaping and laughing into the light, and spread at our feet into a broad bright shallow, in which the kine are standing knee-deep already, a hint, alas! that the day means heat. And there, to the initiated eye, is another and a darker hint of glaring skies, perspiring limbs, and empty creels. Small fish are dimpling in the central eddies; but here, in six inches of water, on the very edge of the ford road, great tails and back-fins are showing above the surface, and swirling suddenly among the tufts of grass, sure sign that the large fish are picking up a minnow-breakfast at the same time that they warm their backs, and do not mean to look at a fly for many an hour to come.

Yet courage; for on the rail of yonder wooden bridge sits, chatting with a sun-browned nymph, her bonnet pushed over her face, her hayrake in her hand, a river-god in coat of velveteen, elbow on knee and pipe in mouth, and rising when he sees us, lifts his wideawake, and holloas back a roar of comfort to our mystic adjuration, –

'Keeper! Is the fly up?'

'Mortal strong last night, gentlemen.'

Wherewith he shall lounge up to us, landing-net in hand, and we will wander up-stream and away.

We will wander – for though the sun be bright, here are good fish to be picked out of sharps and stop-holes – into the water tables, ridged up centuries since into furrows forty feet broad and five feet high, over which the crystal water sparkles among the roots of the rich grass, and hurries down innumerable drains to find its parent stream between tufts of great blue geranium, and spires of purple loosestrife, and the delicate white and pink comfrey-bells, and the avens – fairest and most modest of all the water-side nymphs, who hangs her head all day long in pretty shame, with a soft blush upon her tawny cheek. But at the mouth of each of those drains, if we can get our flies in, and keep ourselves unseen, we will have one cast at least. For at each of them, on some sharp-rippling spot, lies a great trout or two, waiting for beetle, caterpillar and whatsoever else may be washed from among the long grass above. There, and from brimming feeders, which slip along, weed-choked, under white hawthorn hedges, and beneath the great roots of oak and elm, shall we pick out full many a goodly trout. There, in yon stop-hole underneath that tree, not ten feet broad or twenty long, where just enough water trickles through the hatches to make a ripple, are a brace of noble fish, no doubt; and one of them you may be sure of, if you will go the proper way to work, and fish scientifically with the brace of flies which I have put on for you – a governor and a black alder. In the first place, you must throw up into the little pool, not down. If you throw down, they will see you in an instant, and besides, you will never get your fly close under the shade of the brickwork, where alone you have a chance. What use throwing into the still shallow tail, shining like oil in the full glare of the sun?

'But I cannot get below the pool without –'

Without crawling through that stiff shrubbed hedge, well set with trees, and leaping that ten-foot feeder afterwards. Very well. It is this sort of thing which makes the stay-at-home cultivate chalk-fishing as much harder work than mountain angling, as a gallop over a stiffly-enclosed country is harder than one over an open moor. You can do it or not, as you like; but if you wish to catch large trout on a bright day, I should advise you to employ the only method yet discovered.

There, you are through; and the keeper shall hand you your rod. You have torn your trousers, and got a couple of thorns in your shins. The one can be mended, the other pulled out. Now, jump the feeders. There is no run to it, so – you have jumped in. Never mind: but keep the point of your rod up. You are at least saved the lingering torture of getting wet inch by inch and as for cold water hurting anyone –

Now make a circuit through the meadow twenty yards away. Stoop down when you are on the ridge of each table. A trout may be baking at the lower end of the pool, who will see you, rush up and tell all his neighbours. Now, kneel down; take off that absurd black chimney-pot which you are wearing, I suppose, for the same reason as Homer's heroes wore their koruthous and phalerous, to make yourself look taller and more terrible to your foes.

Shorten your line all you can – you cannot fish too short a line up-stream; and throw, not into the oil-basin near you, but right up into the darkest corner. Make your fly strike the brickwork and drop in. – So? No rise? Then, don't work or draw it, or your deceit is discovered instantly. Lift it out, and repeat the throw.

What? You have hooked your fly in the hatches? Very good. Pull at it till the casting-line breaks, put on a fresh one, and to work again. There! you have him. Don't rise! fight him kneeling; hold him hard, and give him no line, but shorten up anyhow. Tear and haul him down to you before he can make to his home, while the keeper runs round with the net . . .There, he is on shore. Two pounds, good weight. Creep back more cautiously than ever, and try again . . .There. A second fish, over a pound weight. Now we will go and recover the flies off the hatches; and you will agree that there is more cunning, more science, and therefore more pleasant excitement, in 'foxing' a great fish out of a stop-hole, than in whipping far and wide over an open stream, where a half-pounder is a wonder and a triumph. And as for physical exertion, you will be able to compute for yourself how much your back, and knees, and fore-arm will ache by nine o'clock to-night, after some ten hours of this scrambling, splashing, leaping, and kneeling upon a hot June day. This item in the day's work will of course be put to the side of loss or of gain, according to your temperament; but it will cure you of an inclination to laugh at us Wessex chalk-fishers as cockneys.

So we will wander up the streams, taking a fish here and a fish there, till – Really it is very hot. We have the whole day before us; and the fly will not be up till five o'clock at least; and then the real fishing will begin. Why tire ourselves beforehand? The squire will send us luncheon in the afternoon, and after that expect us to fish as long as we can, see, and come up to the hall to sleep, regardless of the ceremony of dressing. For is not the green drake on? And while he reigns, all hours, meals, decencies, and respectabilities must yield to his caprice. See, here he sits, or rather tens of thousands of him, one on each stalk of grass. Green drake, yellow drake, brown drake, white drake, each with his gauzy wings folded over his back, waiting for some unknown change of temperature, or something else, in the afternoon, to wake him from his sleep, and send him fluttering over the stream; while overhead the black drake, who has changed his skin and reproduced his species, dances in the sunshine, empty, hard and happy, and we will chat over chalk-fishing.

The first thing, probably, on which you will be inclined to ask questions, is the size of the fish in these streams. We have killed this morning four fish averaging a pound weight each. All below that weight we throw in, as is our rule here; but you may have remarked none of them exceeded half a pound; that they were almost all about herring size. The smaller ones I believe to be year-old fish, hatched last spring twelvemonth; the pound fish, two-year olds. At what rate these last would have increased depends very much, I suspect, on their chance of food. The limit of life and growth in cold-blooded animals seems to depend very much on their amount of food. The boa, alligator, shark, pike, and I suppose the trout also, will live to a great age and attain an enormous size, give them but range enough; and the only cause why there are trout of ten pounds and more in the Thames lashers, while one of four pounds is rare here, is simply that the Thames fish has more to eat. Here, were the fish not sufficiently thinned out every year by anglers, they would soon become large-headed, brown, and flabby, and cease to grow. Many a good stream has been spoilt in this way, when a squire has unwisely preferred quantity to quality of fish.

And if it be not the quantity of feed, I know no clear reason why chalk and limestone trout should be so much larger and better flavoured than any others. The cause is not the greater swiftness of the streams; for (paradoxical as it may seem to many), a trout likes swift water no more than a pike does, except when spawning or cleaning afterwards. At those times his blood seems to require a very rapid oxygenation, and he goes to the 'sharps' to obtain it: but when he is feeding and fattening, the water cannot be too still for him. Streams which are rapid throughout never produce large fish; and a hand-long trout, transferred from his native torrent to a still pond, will increase in size at a ten times faster rate. In chalk streams the largest fish are found oftener in the mill-heads than in the mill-tails. It is a mistake, though a common one, to fancy that the giant trout of the Thames lashers lie in swift water. On the contrary, they lie in the very stillest spot of the whole pool, which is just under the hatches. There the rush of the water shoots over their heads, and they look up through it for every eatable which may be swept down. At night they run down to the fan of the pool, to hunt minnow round the shallows; but their home by day is the still deep; and their preference of the lasher pool to the quiet water above is due merely to the greater abundance of food. Chalk trout, then, are large not merely because the water is swift.

Whether trout have not a specific fondness for lime; whether water of some dozen degrees of hardness is not necessary for their development? are questions which may be fairly asked. Yet is not the true reason this – that the soil on the banks of a chalk or limestone stream is almost always rich – red loam carrying an abundant vegetation, and therefore an abundant crop of animal life, both in and out of the water? The countless insects which haunt a rich hay meadow, all know who have eyes to see; and if they will look into the stream they will find the water-world is even richer than the air-world.

Every still spot in a chalk stream becomes so choked with weed as to require mowing at least thrice a year, to supply the mills with water. Grass, milfoil, water crowfoot, hornwort, starwort, horsetail, and a dozen other delicate plants, form one tangled forest, denser than those of the Amazon, and more densely peopled likewise . . .

The four great trout-fly families are, Phryganeæ, Ephemeræ, Sialidæ, Perlidæ; so you have no excuse for telling – as not only cockneys, but really good sportsmen who write on fishing, have done – such fibs as, that the green drake comes out of a caddis-bait, or give such vague generalities as, 'this fly comes from a water-larva.'

These are, surely, in their imperfect and perfect states, food enough to fatten many a good trout: but they are not all. See these

transparent brown snails, Limneæ and Succinæ, climbing about the posts; and these other pretty ones, coil laid within coil as flat as a shilling (Planorbis). Many a million of these do the trout pick off the weed day by day and no food, not even a leech, which swarms here, is more fattening. The finest trout of the high Snowdon lakes feed almost entirely on leech and snail – baits they have none – and fatten till they cut as red as salmon.

Look here too, once more. You see a grey moving cloud about the pebble bed, and underneath that bank. It is a countless swarm of 'sug' or water-shrimp; a bad food, but devoured greedily by the great trout in certain overstocked preserves.

Add to these plenty of minnow, stone-loach, and miller's thumbs, a second course of crayfish, and for one gormandizing week of bliss, thousands of the great greendrake fly; and you have food enough for a stock of trout which surprise, by their size and number, an angler fresh from the mountain districts of the north and west. To such a fisherman the tale of Mr *** of Ramsbury, who is said to have killed in one day in his own streams on Kennet, seventy-six trout, all above a pound, sounds like a traveller's imagination; yet the fact is, I believe, accurately true.

This, however, is an extraordinary case upon an extraordinary stream. In general, if a man shall bring home (beside small fish) a couple of brace of from one to three pounds a piece, he may consider himself as a happy man, and that the heavens have not shone, but frowned, upon him very propitiously.

THE ANGLER'S INVITATION

BY THOMAS TOD STODDART,
AN ANGLER'S RAMBLES (1866)

I.   Come when the leaf comes, angle with me,
Come when the bee hums crossing the lea;
Come with the wild flowers,
Come with the mild showers,
Come when the singing bird calleth for thee!

II.   Then to the stream-side gladly we'll hie,
Where the grey trout glide temptingly by;
Or in some still place,
Over the hill face,
Cast, ever hoping, the magical fly.

III.   Then when the dew falls, homeward we'll speed
To our own loved walls down on the mead;
There, by the bright hearth,
Holding our night mirth,
We'll drink to sweet friendship in need and in deed!

From ANGLING SKETCHES

BY ANDREW LANG (1891)

Andrew Lang (1844–1912) was born in Selkirk, a small town in the
Borders of Scotland where the rivers of Tweed, Ettrick and Yarrow
all provide excellent trout and salmon fishing. Lang liked to think
of himself as an anthropologist and as such he wrote many papers
on subjects that included *The Making of Religion* and *Myth, Ritual
and Religion*. But it is his collections of fairy tales (each volume
named after a colour) that have stood the test of time and which
are still in print today.

Angling Sketches was written in 1891. It is set on the banks of
the river Tweed near Ashiesteil, Sir Walter Scott's first home in the
Borders before he moved to Abbotsford. The 'Wizard' whom Lang
mentions could either be Merlin, whom it is said was buried at
Drummelzier, or it could be Michael Scott (also mentioned in the
William Scrope extract), traveller, scholar, alchemist and, so it was
also believed, practitioner in the black arts.

* * *

THESE ARE THE WATERS WITH WHICH OUR BOYHOOD WAS MAINLY
engaged: it is a pleasure to name and number them. Memory,
that has lost so much and would gladly lose so much more, brings
vividly back the golden summer evenings by Tweedside, when the
trout began to plash in the stillness – brings back the long,
lounging, solitary days beneath the woods of Ashiesteil – days so
lonely that they sometimes, in the end, begat a superstitious
eeriness. One seemed forsaken in an enchanted world; one might
see the two white fairy deer flit by, bringing to us, as to Thomas
Rhymer, the tidings that we must back to Fairyland. Other waters
we knew well, and loved: the little salmon-stream in the west that
doubles through the loch, and runs a mile or twain beneath its
alders, past its old Celtic battle-field, beneath the ruined shell of its

feudal tower, to the sea. Many a happy day we had there, on loch or stream, with the big sea-trout which have somehow changed their tastes, and today take quite different flies from the green body and the red body that led them to the landing-net long ago. Dear are twin Alines, but dearer is Tweed, and Ettrick, where our ancestor was drowned in a flood, and his white horse found, next day, feeding near his dead body, on a little grassy island. There is a great pleasure in trying methods, in labouring after the delicate art of the dry fly-fisher in the clear Hampshire streams, where the glassy tide flows over the waving tresses of crow's foot below the poplar shade. But nothing can be so good as what is old, and, as far as angling goes, is practically ruined, the alternate pool and stream of the Border waters, where

> The triple pride
> Of Eildon looks over Strathclyde,

and the salmon cast murmurs hard by the Wizard's grave. They are all gone now, the old allies and tutors in the angler's art – the kind gardener who baited our hooks; the good Scotch judge who gave us our first collection of flies, the friend who took us with him on his salmon-fishing expedition, and made men of us with real rods, and 'pirns' of ancient make. The companions of those times are scattered, and live under strange stars and in converse seasons, by troutless waters. It is no longer the height of pleasure to be half-drowned in Tweed, or lost on the hills with no luncheon in the basket. But, except for scarcity of fish, the scene is very little altered, and one is a boy again, in heart, beneath the elms of Yair, or by the Gullets at Ashiesteil. However bad the sport, it keeps you young, or makes you young again, and you need not follow Ponce de Léon to the western wilderness, when in any river you knew of yore, you can find the Fountain of Youth.

From RECOLLECTIONS OF
FLY FISHING

BY EDWARD HAMILTON (1884)

A T TIMES WHEN FISH ARE RUNNING UP FRESH FROM THE SEA IT IS wonderful what freaks they are up to; throwing themselves upwards or sideways, turning somersaults, making tremendous rushes and yet not sporting a bit.

One evening on the Lochy I was returning from the upper part of No 6 beat to have one more cast over the Sloggan when just above the Fox Hunter's cottage the river became suddenly about in all directions. I waded in and cast over hundreds; not a fish would come at the fly, but they would, in their jumps, hit the line often enough.

After a change or two of flies I gave it up and went on my way to the Sloggan. The first cast there with the same fly I had endeavoured to entice the running fish with, I hooked and landed a bright, fresh-run salmon of 10lb.

THE FISHERMAN'S LEGENDARY
KINDNESS

BY JOHN WHITNEY (1700)

In *Surrey* Rises there,
A branch of *Medway*, where
Store of all sorts of Fish do breed,
To serve for Pleasure and for need,
Well stor'd with Game the Rivers be,
Could they from poaching be kept free:

Once Angling at the Rivers side,
Observing how the stream
In gentle motions then did slide,
With eager haste to meet his bride,
And makes his Joys supream;
By chance I spy'd a Rustick Clown,
A halling something up and down,
To him I streight repair,
Aud ask'd his business there.
He told me Fishing for an hour or two,
Lord, how amaz'd was I to see him go,
A bush pul'd from the hedg, his Angling rod
No top, but like a staff with which Men plod,
When driving home full udders to the pail,
Heaven bless me when such tackling can prevail:
His hook ti'd to a string, that to a piece of leather,
A flote just in the place where both were knit together,
Fortune her self that time was double blind,
She could not see and so perforce was kind.
For straight he took to *Bleaks*, one *Roach*,
And last of all a well grown *Perch*,
Who gasping lay upon the ground,
I Judged to weigh at least a pound.
Pleas'd with the fancy I unto him gave,
An Angle, Rod and Line the best I have,
And shew'd him where good baits to find
A Cow-turd, ten days old, and newly lin'd,
With *blew-tails* which from homed *Gentiles* spring,
A ready bait and good for every thing,
The Man was Civil, and exprest his mind,
In real thanks, then sought some better luck to find.

From WILD SPORTS IN IRELAND

BY JOHN BICKERDYKE (1895)

NOW THERE IS NOTHING REMARKABLE ABOUT SEEING A ROD AND reel in Ireland, but these particular weapons made me open my eyes and mouth in amazement. The rod at its point was thick as my little finger, the reel not less than 8in in diameter, and the line – shades of Izaak Walton! What a line was there. I have towed a canoe up the Thames with cord less thick.

I was on the point of enquiring into the particular uses of this remarkable tackle, when the door of the cabin opened and a short, wiry old man with deep set, piercing eyes, iron-grey hair and clad in a shabby suit of tweeds, came in wearily, bearing just another rod and reel, and a huge basket which I instinctively felt contained fish. He took no notice of me, but gasped out, a voice which told of his exhausted condition: 'The steelyard, the steelyard.'

With trembling hands he opened the rush basket and turned out of it one of the largest pike I had ever seen. Mrs O'Day who seemed in no way surprised, produced an ancient rusty instrument and proceeded in a businesslike manner to weigh the fish. The old man's excitement while she did this was painful to witness.

'Is it? Is it?' he commenced.

'No, it isn't,' said Mrs O'Day calmly. 'He's 5lb short.'

I was looking at the fish, but, hearing a groan, turned my eyes to the old fisherman and saw him lying on the floor of the shebeen. He had fainted.

'Poor ould man,' said Mrs O'Day. 'It's disappointed he is and weak too for devil a bit of food has he touched this day since yesterday. Undo his collar sir, and I'll mix him a timperance drink.'

And so her tongue ran on. Meanwhile the old fellow came to himself and sat up, but his eyes went at once to the pike, which still lay on the floor.

'Only 35lb,' I heard him mutter to himself. 'But I will have him soon. I will have him soon now.'

Mrs O'Day's 'timperance' drink was in the nature of an egg flip. It acted like a charm on the old man, who five minutes after drinking it rose, kicked the fish to the side of the cabin and for the first time appeared to be aware that a stranger was in the shebeen. Mrs O'Day noticed the questioning look he cast me.

'It's a gentleman who lost his way in the bog,' she said.

'Not fishing?' he asked rather anxiously.

'No, snipe shooting,' said I, and he seemed to me greatly relieved at the intelligence.

Mrs O'Day now turned out the stew on to a large dish and apologized for having no plates, remarking that she was 'not used to the gentry'. We were both of us more or less famished and talked little during the meal, after which Mrs O'Day having provided us with a second edition of the 'timperance' drink, we drew the settle close to the peat fire, and commenced to chat over our pipes.

My new acquaintance, from what I could gather, was an Englishman who had lived for many years in Ireland and apparently passed his whole time in fishing. But I was able to tell him of certain modern methods of pike fishing of which he had heard nothing. By and by he began to get communicative and finally I ventured to ask him why the weighing of the pike had so disturbed him. Without hesitation he told me the following story.

'From a boy I was an enthusiastic fisherman. I need not trouble to tell you how I caught salmon in Norway, trout in the Test, and enormous grayling in the Hampshire Avon. I fished whenever and wherever I could and nothing, however large or however small, came amiss to me. But one thing I had never caught – a really large pike. Even in Sweden I never took one over 30lb. This nettled me, for many were the tales I read of monsters, particularly in the Irish lakes.

'One morning I read in a sporting paper a letter from an Irishman – a tackle dealer so I afterwards ascertained – asking why English anglers did not come more over there. In the lakes in his neighbourhood there was fine pike fishing. Thirty-pounders were common, and they got a forty-pounder or two every season. Here was exactly the information I wanted. I told some friends about it, but they only smiled. I said I would catch a forty-pounder before long. They replied that there was no such thing as a forty-pounder, alive or stuffed. Well, the end of it was I made a bet that I would go to Ireland and before I returned I would catch a fish of that weight.'

I here interrupted his story to tell him of a strange coincidence. It was that very tacklemaker's letter which had first brought me to Ireland. 'But go on,' I said, 'finish your story and then you shall have mine.'

'I began badly,' he continued, 'I wrote to the man for details of these loughs he mentioned and received a reply from his widow, he having died soon after writing the paragraph. From the poor woman I could get no information. She said she had no idea to which waters her husband referred; in fact, she knew of none. Then I put a letter of enquiry in the sporting papers and received many replies from persons, some of whom were possibly not altogether disinterested in the matter.'

'I have suffered in the same way myself,' I interjected.

'I came to Ireland armed with tackle such as would hold the largest pike that ever lived . . ..' He continued, not noticing my interruption. 'At first I was hopeful. What tales they told me to be sure. There was one of the big pike caught in Lough Derg or, I should say, was killed by some workmen who were digging drains near the lake. The bishop of Killaloe was reputed to be fond of the pike, and to him the fish was taken. It was so large that half its body dragged on the ground as two men carried it, slung on a pole, to the bishop's palace. "I am fond of pike," said he, "but distinctly decline to have anything to do with sharks." Ah! What would I not have given to have caught that fish.

'Well I fished here and I fished there, first trying all the large Shannon Lakes, and then visiting Corrib and Cullen. Thence I went to the north of Ireland, catching now and then some fine fish, but never even a thirty-pounder. The more difficult I found it to attain my object, the more determined I became to succeed. And I shall succeed yet. Let me see. It is now twenty-five years since I came to Ireland. I must have caught thousands of pike in that time – that one there on the floor is the largest of the lot; in fact, the largest I have seen caught by myself or anybody else. This is my second great disappointment. At Athlone I thought I had succeeded. That was a big fish. I took him to the station and weighed him there. "Forty-three pounds," said the station master.

'A Major Brown who was looking on began to prod the fish with his stick. "Something hard there," he said. "Let's cut him open and see what he had for dinner."

'I would not agree to this as I wanted the skin entire, but the major squeezed him a bit and up came a lot of swan shot which my scoundrel of a boatman had evidently poured down his throat so that he might earn the reward I had promised him if I caught a heavy fish.

'But at last I really have found a monster pike – the catching of him is only a question of time. Not a quarter of a mile from this cabin (here he lowered his voice to a whisper) is a deep reedy lake. The priest has a boat on it, which he lends me. I was rowing along the other evening when something struck the boat with such force that I was thrown from the seat and nearly capsized. It was in deep water and there are no rocks in the lake. I had rowed right on to a pike as large as a calf.'

He said the last sentence slowly and earnestly. I expect I showed great interest in the statement for, like the old man, it had long been my ambition to catch a really immense pike.

'Well,' said I, 'let us go and try the lake together. I should like to help you land such a monster.'

'Ah, but you might catch him and not I. How then?' And he gave me a very unpleasant look out of his deep-set eyes.

We said nothing for a while, when my companion suddenly startled me by asking if I was aware that he was the Emperor of Germany. I said I was not, and another unpleasant silence ensued.

Mrs O'Day had made up two heather beds for us on the mud floor and without undressing we each stretched ourselves on our moorland couches.

Just as I was dropping off to sleep, my companion got up on

his elbow and said gravely: 'Hang me if I don't believe you are a pike. I'll have a triangle into you tomorrow morning. Good night.'

There was no doubt about it. He was mad. I dared not go to sleep. I made a pretence of it until the old man began to snore and then sat by the fire until daybreak when, leaving some money on the table for Mrs O'Day, I sped away over the moor.

Years afterwards I was telling the tale of the demented angler who, I felt certain, had lost his wits in his unavailing search after a big Irish pike when I was interrupted by Rooney, of the Irish Bar, who burst into a peal of laughter, swearing that he knew my pike-fishing acquaintance well and that there was no saner man in Ireland.

'Fact is, Johnny,' said he, 'the old boy was fearful you would get that big fish before him and so he thought he would frighten you home.'

Rooney may say what he likes, but I decline to believe in the sanity of any man who expatriates himself during a quarter of a century in the endeavour to catch a 40lb pike.

From FLY FISHING

BY EDWARD GREY (1899)

Sir Edward Grey, Viscount Grey of Fallodon (1862–1933), was a politician and diplomat of some note, and Chancellor of Oxford University from 1928. His two great loves were ornithology and fishing, and he published *Fly Fishing*, from which the following extract is taken, in 1899. Some people consider it the best fishing book ever written, but whatever your view there's no doubt that Grey was an excellent an gler.

* * *

AND NOW LET THE SEASON BE SOMEWHERE ABOUT THE MIDDLE OF May, and let there be a holiday and the angler be at the Test or the Itchen, and let us consider a day's fishing, which shall be typical of many days in this month. The wind shall be south-west, a perceptible breeze, but with no squalls or rough manners; and there shall be light clouds moving before it between which gleams of sunshine fall upon the young leaves and woods – for there are many fine woods by the sides of water meadows. Granted these first two conditions, it will follow that the day is warm, with a temperature reaching 62° in the shade, the mean temperature for midsummer, but a very suitable maximum for a day in May. It is almost certain that there will be a rise of trout at some time during the day, and it is all important to know at what hour it will begin. The chances in my experience are something as follows: It is not certain that there will be no rise before ten o'clock, but it is very improbable that there will be any. After ten o'clock the rise may begin at any time. The most likely time for it is between eleven and twelve, but there need be no disappointment if it does not begin till twelve o'clock. On a day such as this I do, however, become anxious if at one o'clock there is still no rise. Taking then these chances into consideration, desiring earnestly not to miss a minute of the rise, and leaving a fair margin for uncertainties, the angler will probably be at the water by 9.30.

If this forecast of the time of the rise proves correct, and there is at first neither fly nor fish to be seen, the angler has at any rate the satisfaction of feeling that the day is all before him, and that he has so far missed nothing. If he is very impatient to have an outlet at once for his energy, he may put on a medium-sized hackle fly and use it wet in the rough water of hatch-holes, but he can do good – and perhaps he may do some harm – by attempting to fish the river at large. Even in the hatch-holes he will probably prick more fish than he hooks, and if one or two are landed they will either be small trout, or large ones in inferior condition. The fact is, that attempts to anticipate success in a chalk stream before the proper rise begins are unsatisfactory; however resolutely the angler may have made up his mind to expect nothing from these attempts, yet if he labours at them, some sense of disappointment will insensibly steal over him, and take just a little of the edge off his keenness. In my opinion, it is better to keep this unimpaired till the

rise begins. It is not
hard to wait for an
hour or two on
such a day; one
need only
watch and
listen to the
life about the
river. To read a
book at this time is not so easy,
for the eyes are continually being lifted to
the water. On the other hand, there is not
much to be gained by wandering up and
down, and the best plan is for the angler to
go to the lowest part of the water he means to fish, and there sit
down to watch some particular bit of it, which is known to be a
good place for free rising trout. The first sign of the coming rise
will be a few flies upon the water, either olive duns or some near
relations of theirs. These are generally noticed by the angler before
the fish begin to take them, but sometimes it is a trout which first
notices a fly, and then a rise is the first sign seen. When this is so,
the angler becomes alert at once. The pleasure of the day began for
him, let us hope, hours ago, when he woke to the consciousness of
what sort of day it was; but now there is suddenly added to his
happiness the delight of endeavour and excitement, suspense ends,
action begins, and hope is raised to the height of expectation. He
does not, however, cast at once, but gets quietly within reach,
kneeling if necessary to be out of sight, and waiting for the fish to
rise again. This first trout should at any rate be risen, if it is in a
convenient place where the fly does not drag. In a little time it may
have made up its mind not to take any flies on the surface, or its
appetite may have become less keen, or its sense of what all natural
flies look like more exact; but just at first, at the very beginning of
the rise, there is most probability of finding it hungry and off its
guard. By the time the first fish is done with, it should be easy to
find others rising, and if there is a free rise and plenty of fly, the

angler will in May get the best conditioned fish in comparatively quick running water in the main stream. The first half-hour will decide what kind of rise there is to be, whether it is to be a good taking one or not: if it is a good one, the angler should feel for the next two hours that there is at any rate a fair chance of his having a rise whenever he can succeed in floating his fly satisfactorily and accurately over a rising trout. Should the rise last as much as four hours, it is a long one and ought to result in an exceptionally heavy basket. I have generally found, however, that in the last hour or so of the rise the trout become very fastidious and particular. Sometimes they can be seen still in their feeding places, keeping close to the surface of the water, but only taking a fly occasionally, and the angler may, till he is weary, float his own fly over them continually and get no response whatever. As a rule, on a fairly warm day the rise of fly will be over by three or four o'clock. The trout will by then have disappeared, and the angler may leave off. Bad luck or good luck may have made the difference of one or two brace to his basket, but ten pounds' weight of trout should make him content, fifteen pounds may be considered very good, and twenty pounds and upwards exceptional.

The number of trout in different parts of the Itchen and Test is in inverse proportion to their weight; but in parts of these rivers where the trout are not overcrowded and average from a pound and a half to two pounds, they rise freely and their appearance in a good season is splendid. The extraordinary fatness to which they attain, and the brilliancy of their colour and condition in May, June and July, surpass anything it has been my good fortune to see amongst river trout, and anything I could have believed, if I had fished only in north country rivers. On the other hand, the chalk stream trout do not fight so strongly in proportion to their size as the trout in rocky or swifter rivers with rougher water and no weeds. It is not that the southern trout is less strong, but it thinks too much of the weeds: it is always trying to hide itself instead of trying to get free by wild desperate rushes, for which indeed the presence of the weeds and the gentleness of the water make these rivers less suited. Sometimes the first rush of a chalk stream trout when hooked is as sudden and wild and strong as that of a fish of the same size in any other river; but in my experience this generally happens with a south country trout when its feeding place is far down on a shallow or in a long mill-tail, and its home is in the hatch-hole or under the mill above. In such places I have known a trout of one and a half pounds leave very few yards of line upon the reel before its first rush could be checked, and the line to be run out as swiftly and as straight as anyone could wish. Twice during the last season did it happen to me to have fine experiences of this kind. In the first case the trout had something over twenty yards to go for safety, and nearly succeeded. Had the distance been two or three yards less it would have been accomplished in the first rush, but in the last few yards the trout had to collect his strength for a second effort. There was a moment's break in the impetus of the rush, and a struggle began in which at first the trout gained ground, but very slowly, while every foot was contested with the utmost pressure that I dared put upon the gut: then there ceased to be progress, and at last within close sight of his home the trout had to turn his head. The rest was easy, the mill-tail being fairly clear of weeds, and both time and stream being against the fish.

In the second case the result was different. I was wading in a shallow where I could see the trout, which as it turned out, was never to be mine. It was a light-coloured fish feeding actively and recklessly on flies, which were coming down freely, and it took my fly at once with perfect confidence. It sometimes happens, however, that these active, reckless, easily hooked trout are more surprised and desperate when hooked than any others. I never saw anything more mad and sudden than the rush of this trout. It gained a pool below some hatches, where no doubt it lived, and took the line under the rough main stream into a fine whirling back-water: then I felt the confusion of having lost touch with the fish, for there was nothing but the dull sodden strain of a line hopelessly drowned in the contending currents of the hatch-hole. The trout jumped high in the middle of the pool, and showed me that, if under two pounds, he was certainly very thick and strong; I dropped the point of the rod without being able to give the least relief to the fine gut at the end, and the stream swept downwards a useless length of submerged line without a fly.

Those anglers, who are used to thinking that a day's fishing means fishing all day, may ask whether it does not make the pleasure less when the actual fishing is concentrated into a space of sometimes only two, and at most four or five hours, as is the case on a chalk stream in the month of May. The answer is, that the pleasure and excitement are highly concentrated too, and that the work while it lasts is very hard. To be amongst plenty of large trout, with a small fly and fine gut, when there is a good rise, is a glorious experience. Before it is over the angler will have had thrilling and exciting incidents, enough to provide much reflection, and let us hope satisfaction too, and if the rise lasted all day we should be apt to miss much of the glory of the month.

There is so much to be seen and heard in May. There are the separate and successive greens of the fresh young leaves of different trees, perhaps the most tender and the most transient of all the colours that leaves or flowers give to any season. Then there are the great blossoms of May, of which I especially value six, all so conspicuous in colour as to compel one's attention, and three of them wonderful in perfume. They are the lilac, hawthorn, gorse, horse-chestnut, laburnum and broom. Not to spend time in the country while all these things are at their best, is to lead a dull life indeed; and yet, if we are not to miss some of them, we must spend a part at least of every week of May in going about the country with attention free and eyes afield. Dry fly fishing leaves many hours free for this. The first half of May, too, is the most favourable time for making discovery of birds. The summer birds have nearly all arrived, and all birds are singing; but the leaves are not thick yet, and both in brushwood and in trees it is comparatively easy to see the different species. They are active with the business and excitement of the breeding season, and it is just at this time that they most attract the notice of eye and ear. A little later on the air will still be full of sound and song, but it will be much more difficult owing to the leaves to get a good sight of any bird that has attracted attention or raised a doubt of its identity by its song.

May is a good month on a chalk stream, but to my mind the perfection of dry fly fishing is to be had on a good day in mid-June, on water where the May-fly never appears, first to excite the trout and the anglers, and then to leave the fish without appetite and the angler too often discontented. The May-fly is a fine institution, and where it comes in enormous quantities, as it does on some rivers such as the Kennet, it provides a fortnight of most glorious fishing; but elsewhere it interrupts the season, and unless the trout are very large, or there is a great lack of duns and small flies, I would not attempt to reintroduce the May-fly where it has ceased to exist in any numbers.

* * *

In June the trout should be at their very best and strongest, and the angler should be ambitious and go to the water, where he knows there are large ones, to match his skill and his fine gut against them in bright weather. Many a big trout will be seen, risen, and hooked, but the weeds as well as the fish are strong now, and where two-pounders are common and taking well, there are sure to be catastrophes in a long day's fishing. On the other hand, except on very unlucky days, what triumphs there are! what moments of suspense as the fly is floating to the place where one feels sure, either from the sight of the rise or of the very fish itself, that a great trout is feeding! Often in the case of these large trout my rod trembles visibly as the fly comes to the spot, perhaps after all not to be taken. I cannot say which is the more exciting, to have seen only the rise, or to be watching the movement of the fish. The crisis of the rise at one's own fly comes more suddenly when the body of the trout is unseen, but when the fish itself is visible there is a tremendous instant of expectation, as he is seen to prepare to take the fly. The next feeling with me is generally one of downright fear as to where the first rush of the fish will end. This rush may have nothing deliberate about it, in which case all may go well, and in a few seconds the angler may be on equal terms with the fish, and before a minute is over fighting with the odds on his side. On the other hand, there may be in the first rush a horrible set purpose, on the part of the trout, to gain some root under the bank, or to plunge far into a thick bed of weeds, in which case the angler is likely to have the worst of it, for during the first few seconds after being hooked any good conditioned trout of two pounds or upwards can be the master of fine gut. Nor is fine gut the only difficulty: there is another risk owing to the smallness of the hook. It may be possible to succeed with a fairly large imitation of an olive dun on dark days early in the season, but on these days in June a rather small red quill will be the best fly. A small fly, if it is to float well must be tied on a small hook, and a small hook, unless it should fasten in an extra tough part of the mouth, can have but a weak hold of the fish. The angler must therefore be prepared to lose a large fish every now and then – oftener probably than he thinks quite consistent with good luck – by the hook losing its hold. In this matter of losing fish we are more at the mercy of luck in June than in May, and there are times when the luck seems so bad as to turn what promises to be a record day into a comparatively poor one. Sometimes this luck comes in runs. I remember on one day in the height of the summer having, with small red quills and fine gut, the best and the worst luck combined. There were not great numbers of fish feeding, and the trout that were rising were not rising fast. It took a little patience to find a rising fish, and then more patience to fix its exact position by waiting for its next rise. When these things were discovered, however, each fish took my fly confidently, and it seemed as if only the biggest and fattest trout were rising. With each of the first seven fish hooked there was a moment when a catastrophe seemed imminent, and yet all were landed. They averaged just over two pounds apiece, and after each one the sense of triumph and success mounted higher, till it produced a feeling of confidence in my own skill and luck, which I knew was not justified, but which was irresistible. Then everything changed and one disaster succeeded another. I lost more than seven large trout successively. Some broke my tackle, in the case of others the small hook lost its hold unexpectedly, whilst others again went into weeds and there freed themselves from the hook. Indeed I had a very bad time all around. At the end of the rise my basket was heavy, but I had a sense of being much chastened, and I could have wished that the luck had been more evenly distributed.

After two o'clock on this June day the angler will probably find that it becomes increasingly difficult to find a rising trout, and that when one is found, it is not nearly so ready to take his fly. By working hard all the afternoon he may add a brace more to his basket, and he must decide for himself whether this extra brace is worth two or three hours of watching and walking and crawling and kneeling and effort. If he has done pretty well by two o'clock, and if the rise has then become very slack, he may find it more pleasant to leave off for a few hours and arrange the rest of his day so as to come fresh and strong and keen to the evening rise. One difficulty about the evening rise is to settle the time for dining. After various experiments I have found it best to have dinner, if possible, between five and six. Two conditions are essential for this, one is, that there should be some place near the river where dinner can be had, and the other, that the angler should not have eaten much luncheon. The latter of these conditions is not only always possible, but easy out of door: the former one is generally present on the Itchen or Test, where numerous villages with inns are to be found all along the river valleys. Having dined, the angler can call the whole of the long June evening his own, and may enjoy that sense of perfect freedom, strength and patience which is so valuable, and which in fishing is destroyed by hunger or the thought of a fixed dinner hour ahead.

I must own that I do not appreciate the evening rise so well as that in the morning; and there are various reasons for this. In the first place, there is a more definite limit to the end of the evening rise. It is often nearly eight o'clock when it begins and you know then that the light cannot last for more than an hour. Now part of the charm of the morning rise is the prospect of indefinite length. It may only last a short time, but it may go on for hours, and you feel at the beginning that its possibilities are unknown. There is nothing of this with a late evening rise. On the contrary, you feel in

a hurry because the time must be short. If a rising trout will not
take your fly, you begin to fidget as to whether it will be better to
stick to that fish or to try another, and if half-an-hour passes
without any success, the threat of an absolutely blank evening
makes itself felt. There is a story of a thrifty and anxious
housewife, who used to call her household early on Monday
mornings in terms like these, 'Get up! get up at once! to-day's
Monday, to-morrow's Tuesday, next day's Wednesday, here's half
the week gone and no work done!' It is some such fidgety anxiety
that comes over me, if I do not get a fish soon in the evening rise. I
seem to have the anticipation of complete failure. The time is so
short; the beginning and the end of the rise are so near together,
that failure in the first part seems a presage of failure in the whole.

The *look* of the evening rise is so often the best of it. Numbers
of trout appear to be rising frequently and steadily and confidently,
but when the angler puts them to the test, they disappoint him. On
some evenings the trout cease to rise after an artificial fly has once
been floated over them; on others they continue to rise freely, but
will take nothing artificial, and the angler exhausts himself in
efforts and changes of fly, working harder and more rapidly as he
becomes conscious of the approaching end of the day.

But all evenings are not alike disappointing, and on a warm still
evening in June we may expect some success. A few fish may be
found rising very quietly and unobtrusively at any time after six
o'clock. The angler will probably find that these trout are not
feeding in the same way as they fed in the morning. They may be
the same fish, but their manners and behaviour are different. They
are apparently taking some very small insect, are much more easily
scared, and are apt to rise very short, if they rise at all to an
artificial fly; still they are feeding, and are worth trying for. If the
angler can get one or two of these fish before eight o'clock he will
have done well. Soon after eight the evening rise proper should have
begun. More rises will be seen than at any previous time of the day,
and as the light fades the easier it is to get near the fish, and the
more chance is there of hooking them. Yet in my experience it is
comparatively seldom that one has a really successful evening, and

feels that everything has gone well. Now and then one gets two or three brace, or even more, of good trout, but more often, either because the trout rise short, or because too much time is spent unsuccessfully over a stubborn fish, the angler seems to be always on the point of great success without attaining it.

Anglers differ as to how late the evening fishing should be prolonged. Night fishing with a large wet fly should not be allowed on good dry fly water. It is poor fun to haul out of the river by main force in the dark, on thick gut, a trout that might give good sport in daylight. Before it gets dark, however, there is a half-hour in which it is just possible to see where a fish is rising, but just not possible to see one's fly. It needs both skill and judgement to put an artificial fly properly over a fish in these conditions, but during this half-hour a skilful angler may expect to get a brace of good trout with a floating sedge fly. This is perfectly fair fishing, but it has not the same interest as the finer fishing in better light; it needs skill, and yet it is comparatively clumsy work. The angler strikes at sight of a rise without being sure whether it is to his fly or not. He can, and indeed must, use stronger gut, because, when a trout is hooked, he cannot tell accurately what it is doing, or follow its movements adjusting the strain carefully to the need of each moment as he would do in daylight. In short a great part of all that happens, both before and after he hooks a trout, is hidden from him, and he has in the end to rely more upon force, and less upon skill to land the fish. All this takes away much of the pleasure, and if the day has been a fairly good one, I would rather forgo the last brace than kill them under inferior conditions. On the other hand, if luck has been very bad, or the trout have been particularly exasperating and successful in defeating the angler, or have refused to rise all day, then the sedge fly in the last half-hour of perceptible twilight gives a very satisfactory opportunity of trying to get even with them. After a fair day, however, it seems to me better to leave off when I cease to be able to see a medium-sized quill gnat upon the water at a reasonable distance.

Very pleasant the evening is after a successful day in hot, bright weather in June. Let us suppose that the angler has caught some three brace of trout in the day, and a brace and a half in the evening on good water. He will then have had plenty of interest and excitement, moments of anxiety and even of disappointment, but all contributing at the end to give a delightful satisfactory feeling of successful effort. Some great events, some angling crisis there will have been during the day, to which his thoughts will recur often involuntarily. Some incidents will seem to have been photographed upon his mind, so that he can recall clearly not only the particular things done or seen, but his own sensation at the time. What he thinks about in the evening will not be only of angling, but of the scenes in which he has spent his day. I am often ashamed to think how much passes unnoticed in the actual excitement of angling, but the general impression of light and colour, and surroundings is not lost; some is noted at the time, and some sinks into one's mind unconsciously and is found there at the end of the day, like a blessing given by great bounty to one who was too careless at the time to deserve it. May is the month of fresh leaves and bright shrubs, but June is the month in which the water meadows themselves are brightest. The common yellow iris, ragged robin and forget-me-not make rough damp places gay, and the clear water in the little runnels amongst the grass sparkle in the sun. Of wild shrubs which flower in June, there are two so common that they seem to possess the month and meet the eye everywhere. One is the wild rose, and the other is the elder, and great is the contrast between them. The commonest sort of wild rose is surely the most delicate in the scent, colour, form and character of its flowers, and there is nothing more graceful in nature than the way in which a long spray of wild rose in full blossom offers its beauty to be admired. I am not so fond of the elder; when one is close to it there is a certain stiff thickness about the bush, and a deadness of colour both of leaves and flowers, and the scent is heavy and spiritless. But masses of elder flower at a distance have a fine foamy appearance, and I always feel that they are doing their best to honour the season. Though the sun may be as hot as midsummer, everything in the first half of June seems young and fresh and active. Birds are singing still, and for a week or two it seems as if the best of spring and summer, warmth and songs, luxuriance and freshness, were spread abroad so abundantly that it is almost too much. The cup of happiness is full and runs over. Such may be one's last thoughts in the quiet of approaching night after sounds have ceased, and in the perfect enjoyment of 'that still spirit shed from evening air'.

As June draws to a close, and during the whole of July, the rise during the day becomes more uncertain and feeble. There are many days in July when the dry fly angler spends more time in watching and waiting then in active fishing. His best chance before the evening will be between ten and one o'clock, and though he must be prepared for very light baskets, yet there are mornings in July when trout are to be found feeding slowly and quietly here and there, and when they will take a red quill gnat if it is put to them attractively. I have known days in July, when the result of a morning's fishing has been unexpectedly good, equal in total weight to that of the very best days in other months, and equal also in regard to the size and condition of the individual fish.

In August I have only once had a morning's fishing which could fairly be compared, as regards the total weight of trout landed, with the good days of earlier months, and it always seems to me that the condition of the trout in this month ceases to be quite first-rate. Of September, on dry fly rivers, I have had no experience. Anglers who write of it agree in saying that the trout rise better, but that their condition has fallen off, and that an unduly large proportion of female fish are killed.

From An Open Creel

BY H.T. SHERINGHAM (1910)

Hugh Tempest Sheringham (1876-1930) is widely regarded as one of the greatest writers on fishing, of any century. For long the angling editor of *The Field*, his passion for fishing for any species and in any circumstances, coupled with a wonderful prose style, make his work as fresh to read today as when it was written, while his comments about tackle, techniques, and the behaviour of fish often seem astonishingly modern.

* * *

FLOATS

WHEN ONE IS SETTING OUT TO CONSTRUCT A PHILOSOPHY OF angling it would be proper, I think, to begin with the float, the link which connects the contemplative man with the wonders of the deep. Everybody knows about floats; even the Philistine used them to support his inaccuracies touching the craft and the brethren.

A sound scholar, from whom I was privileged to receive the rudiments of humane letters, a man decidedly of opinion that fishing, for small boys, was an undesirable species of 'loafing', used, I remember, to be particularly severe about the float; it was unfortunate, perhaps, that the word lent itself so kindly to alliteration, for your sound scholar dearly loves a phrase, and if he be a masterful man, is apt to make it not only define a situation but also determine a policy. Happily, there were more ways than one out of the school demesne, and the river bank offered several secluded nooks to which the eye of authority never penetrated. The float of those days was a fat, globular thing, gross in aspect, clumsy in movement, and although its painted cheeks were not unpleasing to the eye, so far as float can ever be legitimately condemned as a symbol of folly, it could. Even in that halcyon time, when fish were still unsuspicious, it needed at least a perch to pull its unwieldy form under, a roach no more than made it wobble. Had the sound scholar based his imputations on the ground of using, not a float, but such a float, I should not now be protesting.

For I readily admit that virtue lies almost wholly in using the right float. Shape is important, and so is colour, and it is pleasant at times to dally with material. I have heard many learned disputations on the respective merits of quills from different birds, one man favouring swan, another goose, a third peacock, and each maintaining his opinion with epic accounts of past sport. But as a rule these disputants are a shade too practical; their floats are for use only, and they make no allowance for the element of beauty which should have its place in consideration.

I used at one time to prodigiously admire a certain slender kind of float, fashioned cunningly out of twin sections of clear quill, amber varnished and silk lapped, and tipped at either end with a slim point of bone. I lavished a good shilling thereon (you can buy an admirable cork float for half that sum), partly out of respect for the ideal, partly from belief in the efficacy of the lovely object in pursuit of roaches. Certainly it rode the stream in dainty fashion, peeping slyly out like some modest naiad, and responding even to that bite, perceived by the men of Lea alone, when a fat old roach makes a round mouth at the bait and sucks it in, only that he may expel it the more emphatically, as a pea-shooter expels a pea. Out of the water, too, that float was a delight; it was pleasant merely to let it hang in the air and see the sunlight captured in its transparent body. Once we had a really great fishing together. It was a glorious August day, and the roach were on the feed in every hole of the backwater, which was a string of holes separated by short gravel shallows. With no more than a loose handful of ground bait scattered broadcast in each hole, and with a good, large, piece of white bread on the hook, we caught roach literally as fast as we could. The water was a clear brown, and it was most fascinating to see, down in the depths, the gleam of a broad side as the rod went up and the hook went home, and afterwards, to be able to follow every movement of the fighting fish. The man who has not yet

played a good roach on gossamer tackle in eight or ten feet of clear
water with the sun on it has a rare pleasure still to come. The roach
that day were beauties, and of the twenty kept, three would have
weighed two pounds apiece, had I trusted to instinct and not a
spring balance which had neither heart nor soul, and was (I
maintain it) rusty somewhere inside.

It was shortly after that day that the naiad float disappointed
me by parting asunder at the junction of the two sections of quill,
and leaving me floatless just when the fish were beginning to bite.
The sections could be joined together again, but the float was never
the same after. Sooner or later the water would leak in and the
naiad ceased to be a float, becoming a thing of no classification –
unless it belonged to the order of plummets. On the whole I prefer
my plummets to be of lead, so I gave up the naiad float with a sigh
of regret as a last tribute to its beauty. There remains, however, a
certain habit of mind induced by it, and I still strive after floats
which are good to look at both in line and colour. A slender body
of cork can be very gratifying. For colours give me scarlet above
and green below, with a little knob of sealing-wax at the top of the
quill. This last is for use as well as ornament. The uninitiated
might suppose that nothing could be well more visible to the angler
than the quill's natural white tip sticking out of the water, but what
with the dazzle of sun and flicker of wavelets, it is often very hard
to see, and it is surprising how the little red knob helps the eye.
Properly poised, there is half an inch above water and the half of
this is white, the other half red. When the white has disappeared
you have a noble bite as roach bites go, and you may strike at once.
It is not often that the roach of these degenerate days takes one's
float right down out of sight. For evening fishing, when the last
faint light is on the water, a black-headed float is most visible.

At one time I used to fish occasionally through the dark hours,
and I was mightily puzzled to find a float which I could see after
dark. I tried adding a cone of white paper to the tip, and at first
deluded myself with the idea that it was visible; but when, after
intently watching it for a long time, I discovered that I was really
gazing at nothing, I gave it up. The discovery was due to a horrid

eel, which had taken my float off in a wholly opposite direction. Incidentally that eel very nearly made me give up night fishing also. Let him who doubts, try to unhook an eel among thistles by the light of the stars and a wax match. Later in the same summer, however, I came upon an ancient bream-fisher at dusk, perched on a camp stool, and brooding over the quiet waters like some sad heron. Attached to the top of his float was a feather, blacker than the impending gloom, and therefore visible against the water-line longer than anything else.

A man of few words, that ancient. He may perhaps have been susceptible to the mysteries of night, the rustling and whispering of unseen creatures, the melancholy owls in the woods behind, the low murmur of the restless river, the reflected track of the stars growing even fainter, as dawn approached, to the deathly chill of the darkest hour. But of these things he said nothing; his hope was a sackful of bream before sunrise.

I sometimes pick out of a drawer a queer little black object with a fat white head which I am informed is a 'luminous' float, and so often as I do so I think of that old bream-fisher, sitting solitary through the nights, and wonder whether he ever met the river god face to face.

For my part I never could catch anything to speak of after dark, and the luminous float goes back into the drawer where it has lain all these years unused.

One old writer, by the way, two hundred years ago, commended to his disciples the use of glow-worms imprisoned in a clear quill float, and is minute in his instructions as to getting the best light of them! But I suspect him of depending on tradition rather than on experience. He is more practical when he comes to a floating reed:

'Note, if at any time the angler should be destitute of floats, when he comes to the waterside to angle, and there be 'ere a dry sound reed to be gotten, cut it close the joints, leaving two joints in every float uncut, one at one end, and another at t'other, to keep out of the water; it will make a good float in time of need.'

Float caps are most pleasing when cut out of quill and stained a deep red, but most practical when cut from a length of fine black rubber tubing. A foot of this will last a season through.

You can also embellish your floats yourself if you please. A long swan quill can be given a coat of Lincoln green and a head of crimson with aid of varnish stain or enamel, and it is then sufficiently attractive to be the companion of one's days. The true test of matrimony is said to be continued ability on the part of the persons involved to survey each other across the breakfast-table without weariness. If you consider that the angler has to watch his float motionless, 'a painted ship upon a painted ocean' for hours with no intrinsic interest beyond the float and the watching, you will perceive that a fair appearance has its value here also.

But, of course, one is best pleased with one's float when it vanishes from sight, so I will not seek to press the analogy too closely. Moreover, you can always change your float when you get tired of it, and try another with a new colour scheme. If luck counts for anything, it is sometimes worth doing.

But there is a thing about floats which I have noticed most sorrowfully and cannot explain. The one which looks nicest, and sits best in the water, and reveals most bites, always is to be found on the line of the other man. To comprehend this, one must, I fancy, plumb deeper depths than those of angling.

and from COARSE FISHING

(1913)

CARP

For practical purposes there are big carp and small carp. The latter you may sometimes hope to catch without too great a strain on your capabilities. The former – well, men *have* been known to catch them, and there are just a few anglers who have caught a good many. I myself have caught one, and I will make bold to repeat the talk of the adventure as it was told in *The Field* of July 1, 1911.

The narrative contains most of what I know concerning the capture of big carp. The most important thing in it is the value which it shows to reside in a modicum of good luck.

So far as my experience goes, it is certain that good luck is the most vital part of the equipment of him who would seek to slay big carp . . .

And so to my story. I had intended to begin it in a much more subtle fashion, and only by slow degrees to divulge the purport of it, delaying the finale as long as possible, until it should burst upon a bewildered world like the last crashing bars of the *1812* Overture.

But I find that, like Ennius (though without his justification for a somewhat assured proceeding) *volito vivus per ora virum*. Now that a considerable section of the daily press has taken cognisance of the event, it is no good my delaying the modest confession that I have caught a large carp. It is true. But it is a slight exaggeration to state that the said carp was decorated with a golden ring bearing the words '*Me valde dilexit atque ornavit propter immensitatem meam Issachius Walton, anno Domini MDCIII.*'

Nor was it the weightiest carp ever taken. Nor was it the weightiest carp of the present season. Nor was it the weightiest carp of June 24. Nor did I deserve it. But enough negation. Let me to the story which will explain the whole of it.

To begin with, I very nearly did not go at all because it rained furiously most of the morning. To continue, towards noon the face of the heavens showed signs of clearness and my mind swiftly made itself up that I would go after all. I carefully disentangled the sturdy rod and the strong line, the triangle hooks, and the other matters which had been prepared the evening before, and started armed with roach tackle. The loss of half a day had told me that it was vain to think of big carp. You cannot of course fish for big carp in half a day. It takes a month.

I mention these things by way of explaining why I had never before caught a really big carp, and also why I do not deserve one now. As I have said, I took with me to Cheshunt Lower Reservoir roach tackle, a tin of small worms, and intention to try for perch, with just a faint hope of tench. The natural condition of the water is weed, the accumulated growth of long years. When I visited it for the first time some eight years ago I could see nothing but weed, and that was in mid-winter. Now, however, the Highbury Anglers, who have rented the reservoir, have done wonders towards making it fishable. A good part of the upper end is clear, and elsewhere there are pitches cut out which make excellent feeding grounds for fish and angling grounds for men. Prospecting, I soon came to the forked stick, which has a satisfying significance to the ground-baitless angler. Someone else had been there before, and the newcomer may perchance reap the benefit of another man's sowing. So I sat me down on an empty box thoughtfully and began to angle. It is curious how great, in enclosed water especially, is the affinity between small worms and small perch. For two hours I struggled to teach a shoal of small perch that hooks pull them distressfully out of the water.

It was in vain. Walton must have based his 'wicked of the world' illustration on the ways of small perch.

I had returned about twenty and was gloomily observing my float begin to bob again when a cheery voice, that of Mr. R. G. Woodruff, behind me, observed that I ought to catch something in that swim. I had certainly fulfilled the obligation; and it dawned on me that he was not speaking of small perch, and then that my rod was resting on the forked stick and myself on the wood box of the Hon. Secretary of the Anglers' Association. He almost used force to make me stay where I was, but who was I to occupy a place so carefully baited for carp, and what were my insufficient rod and flimsy line that they should offer battle to 10-pounders? Besides, there was tea waiting for me, and I had had enough of small perch.

So I made my way for the rightful owner of the pitch, but not before he had given me good store of big lobworms, and also earnest advice to try for carp with them, roach rod or no roach rod. He told me of a terrible battle of the evening before when a monster took his worm in the dark and also his cast and hook. Whether it travelled north or south he could hardly tell in the gloom but it travelled far and successfully. He hoped that after the rain there might be a chance of a fish that evening.

Finally, I was persuaded that during tea I looked out a strong cast and a perch hook on fairly stout gut, and soaked them in the teapot till they were stained a light brown. Then, acquiring a loaf of bread by good fortune, I set out to fish. There were plenty of other forked sticks here and there which showed where other members had been fishing, and I finally decided on a pitch at the lower end, which I remembered from the winter as having been the scene of an encounter with a biggish pike that got off after a considerable fight. There, with a background of trees and bushes, some of whose branches made handling a 14-foot rod rather difficult, it is possible to sit quietly and fairly inconspicuous. And there accordingly I sat for three hours and a quarter, watching a float which only moved two or three times when a small perch pulled the tail of the lobworm, and occupying myself otherwise by making pellets of paste and throwing them out as ground bait.

Though fine it was a decidedly cold evening, with a high wind; but this hardly affected the water, which is entirely surrounded by a high bank and a belt of trees. Nor was there much to occupy the attention except when some great fish would roll over in the weeds far out, obviously one of the big carp, but a hundred yards away. An occasional moorhen and a few rings made by small roach were the only signs of life. The black tip of my float about eight yards away, in the dearth of other interests began to have an almost hypnotising influence. A little after half-past eight this tip trembled and then disappeared and so intent was I on looking at it that my first thought was a mild wonder as to why it did that. Then the coiled line began to go through the rings, and I realized that here was a bite.

Rod in hand, I waited until the line drew taut, and struck gently. Then things became confused. It was as though some submarine suddenly shot out into the lake. The water was about six feet deep, and the fish must have been near the bottom, but he made a most impressive wave as he dashed straight into the weeds about twenty yards away, and buried himself in them. And so home, I murmured to myself, or words to that effect, for I saw not the slightest chance of getting a big fish out with a roach rod and fine line. After a little thought, I decided to try hand-lining, as one does for trout, and getting hold of the line – with some difficulty because the trees prevented the rod point going far back – I proceeded to feel for the fish with my hand.

At first there was no response; the anchorage seemed immovable. Then I thrilled to a movement at the other end of the line which gradually increased until the fish was on the run again, pushing the weeds aside as he went, but carrying a great streamer or two with him on the line. His run ended, as had the first, in another weed patch, and twice after he seemed to have found safety in the same way. Yet each time hand-lining was efficacious, and eventually I got him into the strip of clear water; here the fight was an easier affair, though by no means won. It took, I suppose, some fifteen or twenty minutes before I saw a big bronze side turn over, and was able to get about half the fish into my absurdly small net. Luckily by this time he had no fight left in him, and I dragged him safely up the bank and fell upon him. What he weighed I had no idea, but I put him at about twelve pounds, with a humble hope that he might be more.

At any rate, he had made a fight that would have been considered very fair in a twelve-pound salmon, the power of his runs being certainly no less and the pace of them quite as great. On the tackle I was using, however, a salmon would have fought longer.

The fish knocked on the head, I was satisfied, packed up my tackle, and went off to see what the other angler had done. So far he had not had a bite, but he meant to go on as long as he could see, and hoped to meet me at the train. He did not do so, for a very good reason; he was at that moment engaged in a grim battle in the darkness with a fish that proved ultimately to be one ounce heavier than mine, which, when weighed on the scales at the keeper's cottage, was sixteen pounds five ounces. As I owe him my fish, because it was his advice that I put on the strong cast, and the bait was one of his lobworms, he might fairly claim the brace. And he would deserve them, because he is a real carp fisher and has taken great pains to bring about his success. For myself – well, luck attends the undeserving now and then. One of them has the grace to be thankful.

HEAVEN

BY RUPERT BROOKE (1914)

Rupert Chawner Brooke (1887–1915) is mostly remembered for his poetry of the First World War – the best of which captured the romantic patriotism of the early war years before it turned to disillusionment. Both the poems included in this anthology also reveal Brooke to be a great lover of the English countryside. They capture the 'fishiness' of fish in the most limpid of images. Sadly Brooke was lost to the literary world when he died – of blood poisoning – in the Aegean on the way to fight in the Dardanelles. He was buried on the island of Scyros on 23 April 1915.

* * *

Fish (fly-replete, in depth of June
Dawdling away their wat'ry noon)
Ponder deep wisdom, dark or clear,
Each secret fishy hope or fear.
Fish say, they have their Stream and Pond;
But is there anything Beyond?
This life cannot be All, they swear,
For how unpleasant, if it were!
One may not doubt that, somehow, Good
Shall come of Water and of Mud;
And, sure, the reverent eye must see
A Purpose in Liquidity.
We darkly know, by Faith we cry,
The Future is not Wholly Dry.
Mud unto mud! – Death eddies near –
Not here the appointed End, not here!
But somewhere, beyond Space and Time,
Is wetter water, slimier slime!
And there (they trust) there swimmeth One

Who swam ere rivers were begun,
Immense, of fishy form and mind,
Squamous, omnipotent, and kind;
And under that Almighty Fin,
The littlest fish may enter in.
Oh! never fly conceals a hook,
Fish say, in the Eternal Brook,
But more than mundane weeds are there.
And mud, celestially fair;
Fat caterpillars drift around,
And Paradisal grubs are found;
Unfading moths, immortal flies,
And the worm that never dies.
And in that Heaven of all their wish,
There shall be no more land, say fish.

From Big Two-Hearted River

by Ernest Hemingway (1925)

For anyone asked to name an American novelist of the earlier part of the twentieth century Ernest Hemingway (1899–1961) is probably the first to come to mind. His best-known works, such as *A Farewell to Arms* and *For Whom the Bell Tolls* have been made into films. Based in Paris, he actively supported the Republicans during the Spanish Civil War and became a war correspondent in Europe during the Second World War. He had a passion for bullfighting, which was probably part of his deliberate cultivation of brutality. That said, the following extract from *Big Two-Hearted River* shows a calmer side to his nature. It is a beautifully measured piece of prose and sums up perfectly the patience one needs to become a good fisherman.

PART II

IN THE MORNING THE SUN WAS UP AND THE TENT WAS STARTING TO get hot. Nick crawled out under the mosquito netting stretched across the mouth of the tent, to look at the morning. The grass was wet on his hands as he came out. He held his trousers and his shoes in his hands. The sun was just up over the hill. There was the meadow, the river and the swamp. There were birch trees in the green of the swamp on the other side of the river.

The river was clear and smoothly fast in the early morning. Down about two hundred yards were three logs all the way across the stream. They made the water smooth and deep above them. As Nick watched, a mink crossed the river on the logs and went into the swamp. Nick was excited. He was excited by the early morning and the river. He was really too hurried to eat breakfast, but he knew he must. He built a little fire and put on the coffee pot.

While the water was heating in the pot he took an empty bottle and went down over the edge of the high ground to the meadow. The meadow was wet with dew and Nick wanted to catch grasshoppers for bait before the sun dried the grass. He found plenty of good grasshoppers. They were at the base of the grass stems. Sometimes they clung to a grass stem. They were cold and wet with the dew, and could not jump until the sun warmed them. Nick picked them up taking only the medium-sized brown ones, and put them into the bottle. He turned over a log and just under the shelter of the edge were several hundred hoppers. It was a grasshopper lodging house. Nick put about fifty of the medium browns into the bottle. While he was picking up the hoppers the others warmed in the sun and commenced to hop away. They flew when they hopped. At first they made one flight and stayed stiff when they landed, as though they were dead.

Nick knew that by the time he was through with breakfast they would be as lively as ever. Without dew on the grass it would take him all day to catch a bottle full of good grasshoppers and he would have to crush many of them, slamming at them with his hat. He washed his hands at the stream. He was excited to be near it.

Then he walked up to the tent. The hoppers were already jumping stiffly in the grass. In the bottle, warmed by the sun, they were jumping in a mass. Nick put in a pine stick as a cork. It plugged the mouth of the bottle enough, so the hoppers could not get out and left plenty of air passage.

He had rolled the log back and knew he could get grasshoppers there every morning.

Nick laid the bottle full of jumping grasshoppers against a pine trunk. Rapidly he mixed some buckwheat flour with water and stirred it smooth, one cup of flour, one cup of water. He put a handful of coffee in the pot and dipped a lump of grease out of a can and slid it sputtering across the hot skillet. On the smoking skillet he poured smoothly the buckwheat batter. It spread like lava, the grease spitting sharply. Around the edges the buckwheat cake began to firm, then brown, then crisp. The surface bubbling slowly to porousness. Nick pushed under the browned under surface with a fresh pine chip. He shook the skillet sideways and the cake was loose on the surface. I won't try and flop it, he thought. He slid the chip of clean wood all the way under the cake, and flopped it over on to its face. It sputtered in the pan.

When it was cooked Nick regreased the skillet. He used all the batter. It made another big flapjack and one smaller one.

Nick ate a big flapjack and a smaller one, covered with apple butter. He put apple butter on the third cake, folded it over twice, wrapped it in oiled paper and put it in his shirt pocket. He put the apple butter jar back in the pack and cut bread for two sandwiches.

In the pack he found a big onion. He sliced it in two and peeled the silky outer skin. Then he cut one half into slices and made onion sandwiches. He wrapped them in oiled paper and buttoned them in the other pocket of his khaki shirt. He turned the skillet upside down on the grill, drank the coffee, sweetened and yellow brown with the condensed milk in it, and tidied up the camp. It was a good camp.

Nick took his fly rod out of the leather rod-case, jointed it, and shoved the rod-case back into the tent. He put on the reel and threaded the line through the guides. He had to hold it from hand to hand, as he threaded it, or it would slip back through its own weight. It was a heavy, double tapered fly line. Nick had paid eight dollars for it a long time ago. It was made heavy to lift back in the air and come forward flat and heavy and straight to make it possible to cast a fly which has no weight. Nick opened the aluminium leader box. The leaders were coiled between the damp flannel pads. Nick had wet the pads at the water cooler on the train up to St Ignace. In the damp pads the gut leaders had softened and Nick unrolled one and tied it by a loop at the end of the heavy fly line. He fastened a hook on the end of the leader. It was a small hook; very thin and springy.

Nick took it from his hook book, sitting with the rod across his lap. He tested the knot and the spring of the rod by pulling the line taut. It was a good feeling. He was careful not to let the hook bite into his finger.

He started down the stream, holding his rod, the bottle of grasshoppers hung from his neck by a thong tied in half hitches around the neck of the bottle. His landing net hung by a hook from his belt. Over his shoulder was a long flour sack tied at each corner into an ear. The cord went over his shoulder. The sack flapped against his legs.

Nick felt awkward and professionally happy with all his equipment hanging from him. The grasshopper bottle swung against his chest. In his shirt the breast pockets bulged against him with the lunch and his fly book.

He stepped into the stream. It was a shock. His trousers clung tight to his legs. His shoes felt the gravel. The water was a rising cold shock.

Rushing, the current sucked against his legs. Where he stepped in, the water was over his knees. He waded with the current. The gravel slid under his shoes. He looked down at the swirl of water below each leg and tipped up the bottle to get a grasshopper.

The first grasshopper gave a jump in the neck of the bottle and went out into the water. He was sucked under in the whirl by Nick's right leg and came to the surface a little way downstream. He floated rapidly, kicking. In a quick circle, breaking the smooth surface of the water, he disappeared. A trout had taken him.

Another hopper poked his face out of the bottle. His antennæ wavered. He was getting his front legs out of the bottle to jump. Nick took him by the head and held him while he threaded the slim hook under his chin, down through his thorax and into the last segments of his abdomen. The grasshopper took hold of the hook with his front feet, spitting tobacco juice on it. Nick dropped him into the water.

Holding the rod in his right hand he let out line against the pull of the grasshopper in the current. He stripped off line from the reel with his left hand and let it run free. He could see the hopper in the little waves of the current. It went out of sight.

There was a tug on the line. Nick pulled against the taut line. It was his first strike. Holding the now living rod across the current, he brought in the line with his left hand. The rod bent in jerks, the trout pumping against the current. Nick knew it was a small one. He lifted the rod straight up in the air. It bowed with the pull.

He saw the trout in the water jerking with his head and body against the shifting tangent of the line in the stream.

Nick took the line in his left hand and pulled the trout, thumping tiredly against the current, to the surface. His back was mottled the clear, water-over-gravel colour, his side flashing in the sun. The rod under his right arm, Nick stooped, dipping his right hand into the current. He held the trout, never still, with his moist right hand, while he unhooked the barb from his mouth, then dropped him back into the stream.

He hung unsteadily in the current, then settled to the bottom beside a stone. Nick reached down his hand to touch him, his arm to the elbow under the water. The trout was steady in the moving stream, resting on the gravel beside a stone. As Nick's fingers touched him, touched his smooth, cool, underwater feeling he was gone, gone in a shadow across the bottom of the stream.

He's all right, Nick thought. He was only tired.

From FAREWELL THOU BUSY WORLD

BY JOHN H. BRADLEY (1935)

FOR THE SUPREME TEST OF A FISHERMAN IS NOT HOW MANY FISH he has caught, not even how he has caught them, but what he has caught when he has caught no fish.

From WHERE THE BRIGHT WATERS MEET

BY HENRY PLUNKETT GREENE (1924)

Like Sir Michael Hordern or Lord Grey of Fallodon, whose work can be found elsewhere in this book, Henry (Harry) Plunkett Greene (1865-1936) was best known not as a fishing writer, but for his success in an entirely different career. Born in Ireland, early recognition that he possessed a fine voice led to him studying singing in Florence, Stuttgart and London, making his first public appearance in Handel's *Messiah* in London in 1888. His career blossomed, and he was especially admired both for his interpretative sense and for his diction, excelling particularly in recitals of lieder and songs. An ardent dry-fly fisherman, he published his *Where the Bright Waters Meet* in 1924, and it has remained a classic ever since.

* * *

FISHING IS A REAL TEST OF CHARACTER. YOUR SPIRITS ARE EITHER on top of a mountain or in the depths of a pit, with certain dead-levels of boredom and commonplace, supposing your soul craves for poundage alone. But there are many sufferings and

humiliations outside the orthodox annoyances of the atrocious
British climate: the fly in the small of your back which you have to
undress yourself to get at; the broken Thermos bottle; the
disintegrated lunch, bulls, wasps' nests, moor-hens at the wrong
moment, cockchafers in your eye, the other man round the corner
at the very spot you have been working up to all morning, the cast
which doubles back, the matches which you have left at home and,
worst of all, water in your waders. Of all the maddening things the
worst is falling into the water. I have fallen into the Spey three
times – near the bank each time, fortunately, for the Spey is in such
a hurry to get you to the sea that it does not give you any time to
stop and think. In fact, I made such a habit of it that I gave up
wearing my watch and left it at home. I was not much the worse for
it except for badly damaging one of my fingers in an attempt to
link up with Mother Earth, but to have your tobacco and cigarettes
made into a wet mush and to feel the icy water trickle gradually
from your waist to your toes is enough to bolshevize a saint,
especially as it means either walking home a couple of miles to
change your things or inviting double pneumonia. The wonder is
that you can wade in the Spey at all. It runs like a mill-race, and the
bottom is covered with rocks varying in size from a parched pea to
a Roman encampment and in shape from a marble to a cubist
portrait. At low water these are covered with slime, and a limpet or
an anemone would slide about on them as on roller-skates. In view
of the precariousness of the foothold and the enthusiasm of the
water, the Spey wader should be equipped with a Gieve waistcoat,
an air-balloon, and a wire hawser attached to a ghillie or a derrick,

on shore,

and should

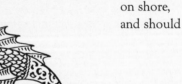

have a portable hot-coffee machine keeping pace with him on the bank with a spare set of clothes in the oven. As it is, he has to put up with a pole with which to prod the immediate future, and which at one moment runs up against the rock of Gibraltar and the next descends into the bowels of Vesuvius.

An Angler's Prayer

Lord, grant that I may catch a fish so big that even I,
When speaking of it afterwards, may have no need to lie.

From Going Fishing

by Negley Farson (1942)

(James Scott) Negley Farson (1890-1960) was a foreign correspondent for the *Chicago Daily News* in the twenties and thirties. A dedicated fisherman, he took his rod wherever he went and thus *Going Fishing* includes some delightful encounters with among other creatures, wild geese in the Carolinas and horses in the Caucasus. Farson also has countless tales to tell of his piscine adventures in such diverse countries as Chile, Norway, France, Scotland and Yugoslavia. His latter years were spent in Devon and the following extract is a prime example of the type of fishing one could expect in that county back in the forties.

Fishing the West Country of England; Reward

THERE IS A SPOT IN THE WEST COUNTRY THAT IS ALMOST A sanctuary for a vanishing type of Englishman. There is not a day in the year when you may not kill something. Stag, hind, fox, otter, rabbits; pheasant, partridge, black-cock, woodcock, snipe, possibly some passing duck – salmon and trout. They all come in their seasons. These seasons overlap so that you may have three or four kinds of different sport in as many days. You may hunt the stag, and the next day be with a shotgun on the rolling green hills; on the next you may take your rod and try the last of the year's fishing. To these sporting Englishmen who live there, a day when something is not killed is a day of frustration, a day wasted.

But Captain Tantivy is not a bloodthirsty man, even if he may act as if he had been put on the earth to kill everything on it. It is not the killing which whips up the blood of this survival of the old English sporting squires. You will never understand Captain Tantivy until you see the aftermath of a hunt. The long ride home with the darkness settling around you. The final barbaric touch of splendour of a rainy, windy sunset over the empty moor. The tired hounds. The pink coat of the huntsman fast turning into just a black silhouette on ahead. This, and the thought of the warm bath, the restful drink, and the cosy fire that awaits you at the pub.

Yes, this, and the picture still in your mind of the 'Tufters' trying to cut a hind out of a herd in a deep stand of wintry beech in the morning, and then a batch of horsemen like an old sporting print coming hell for leather down a sheer slope of dead fern.

'Yagga-yagga-yagga! Hyeah-hyeah-hyeah! Toot-toototoot! . . . Ernest, if you can't read – ye can bloody well hear, can't you! Go back! Go back! Go back! She's turned . . .she's turned . . .ride like hell down the valley! Toot-toot-toot-yagga-yagga-yagga, you – !'

It is perhaps with a deep satisfaction that you see the hind, fleeing for her life, bounding across the deep green farmlands that lie in the valley bottom, soaring over the hedges as if catapulted on springs – deep, deep, deep into another woodland sanctuary. The hound music tingles in your veins. But you will be just as pleased when you get home to see mud-bespattered Captain Tantivy sigh that the hind ran them thirty miles – and then was not killed. For you will know that deep down in his heart Captain Tantivy is also not disconsolate. He has had a grand day. He has fulfilled himself.

That is the exciting side of this country I have been talking about. But it is not the one for which I go there. To me this English scene, where the dark rivers curve down from Exmoor, is the joy of the familiar and the luxury of my own solitude by its river banks.

Of the familiar, I know that I shall find in the tap room the water bailiff who has been on the Exe and Barle for over forty years. What he doesn't know about fish is hardly worth mentioning. Putting down his pipe, he will tell you of how he never eats fish . . . because . . . well, it must have fifteen years ago . . . there was a year when the salmon came up the river with a disease of their gills, and when you took them out of the water they were all soft and spongy. 'And since then I never could bide a fish! I couldn't eat one.'

He will tell you of the flies which are inevitably disappearing – killed by the oil seeping into the water from the tarred roads and motor cars. He hasn't seen a Green Dunham for years. The Red Spinner is getting rare. He wouldn't be surprised if, one day, the old trusty March Brown himself disappeared. Yes, Mr X is dead . . . a pity . . . a fine gentleman, too. The year they took eighty-two salmon out of the river, Mr X caught fifty-four of them. A grand gentleman. It's been a good salmon year, this one, too . . . which means it will be a bad trout year. And when I say to him that I have fished a river along which there just were no motor cars, he will sigh: 'Ay . . . that would be a grand place for the likes of we!'

And Hardy, the rabbit trapper? Well, he hasn't been so 'clever' this last winter; his back, you know. Then they took out all the rest of his teeth. But he'll be at the Lamb . . . or else you'll find him in the Lion.

And Hardy will produce his ferrets. We have stood on the opposite side of those thick sod hedges over many years. Bless his heart, he will bring a handful of ferrets into the Lion! Rosie was shot by a gentleman, who stuffed Rosie back into a hole – and said nothing about it – therefore he was not a gentleman.

'Spent all afternoon trying to find her, I did! But Robin Hood is still alive. So is Fitchie. And here's a new one – Buffalo Bill.'

Hardy picks the three of them up and lets their pink noses touch his cheeks, as if they were kissing him. He has seventeen ferrets this year. And he *can* talk to them; for he would put Rosie into a hole and say: 'Now you run along *inside*, Rosie . . . Father can go along *outside*.' And then you would see Rosie come out, blink at him with her pink eyes, as if asking what to do next!

This is part of the welcome familiar.

This was a long remove from the wild scrub country of southern Chile. It was totally different from the pine forests, and the thundering rivers of Norway I was going to fish that September. It was equally distant, in its character, from the streams of France I was going to fish in Haute Savoie within the next few weeks. But it held something which none of these other scenes could offer.

I think the best thing to call it is a certain quiet decency. This almost unchanging English scene, with its red and green rolling hills, holds a romance that wild rocks, and wild rivers, or snow-capped volcanoes could never give you. It has a gentleness, a rich rustic worth, and an unostentatiousness that is like the English character. An imperturbable scene which fills you with contentment.

You are lucky if the trout you catch here average three to the pound. Very lucky! When you come back to the hotel at night you will find that there are some plates by the door. Two, three, perhaps even ten trout may be lying on a plate. But they are just dinner plates. No salvers needed. And you will put down your own monster – let's say that you have actually caught a half-pounder – with as much quiet satisfaction as you would drop down that six-pounder in southern Chile. In fact, considering the circumstances, you have done an even more wonderful thing.

Here with a little aluminium box in your pocket, or a few flies stuck in your coat lapel, you will fish all day with a cast so fine that it looks like a strand of a brunette's hair. Perhaps it is better to buy your casts and flies from the fishing-fanatic in the little town nearby. He stains his own casts and ties his own flies and is so covered with flies stuck into his coat and hat himself that he looks like a veritable cockleburr. Here is another of the welcome familiars with whom it is as much of a delight to gossip about fish as it is with the water bailiff. More, in fact, because this person, who runs the local bicycle and tackle shop, will leave his shop on the slightest excuse merely to catch a fish. He has, I believe, one or two anonymous flies with which he has experimented himself. But the ones he will probably recommend you are the small hackled blue upright – with most of its hackle snipped off; the Hare's Ear, Pheasant Tail, Greenwell's Glory, and, as the season gets on, the apparently irresistible Little Tup. Then it is a question of where and how you present the flies.

* * *

The gentle art of stream fishing in the West Country of England (I never could afford a rod on a big chalk stream) has a charm all of its own. Perhaps that is just why I have never tried to fish for salmon on this river, although I have certainly fished it double the number of times I have fished any loch or river in Scotland. As I have said, I enjoy the luxury of my own solitude, my own idle reflections – the inner solitude. There are times when I don't want trouble, I don't want thrills; I have come here for just a lazy contentment. Sometimes I do not want to do anything but lie in the sun. Fresh spring days, with the sun hot on the green meadows, when the shadows of the clouds seem to 'peel' off the hills; when the crows are still building their ragged nests in the leafless trees; when the weirs run white from the heavy flow that comes down from where the red deer lie among the bracken on Exmoor; when the sheep are lambing and you lie there, watching the ewes butt the tottering lambs away – the silly ones which don't know their own mothers. The time when the primroses are just about going and soon that little white flower, like a buttercup, will appear . . . growing in rafts above the beds of green waterweeds bending in the slacks of water.

I like to watch the plover, tumbling about in the sky over the red, ploughed fields; and Mr Rat, emerging from his hole and going about his business; the silent, ceaseless flight of the swallows over some shallow stream.

* * *

But then, this is just about the time when you ought to be fishing. There is just the right amount of discoloration in the water. And

you realize, as you wade, that small-river fishing is good for you. It
breaks you of the long, careless cast that loch fishing, or the heavy
river, has got you into. If you are on the shore of a loch you are
always casting to see how far out you can get; the fish must be
there. If you are in a boat you are always trying long casts in among
the rocks along the shore; the fish must be there. If you are in the
middle of a shallow lock you are always trying to drop your flies as
far away as you can from your boat – in case it might have
frightened them. Those are the habits which I, at least, have got
into. You become careless about a slack line; to drop your flies
lightly seems your only consideration. And you play fish too long.

But here, on a little river like this, you have to be canny. It is all
a question of where you put your fly. The shorter your line – and
the time you play your fish – the better. And you have to know
water; the tempting deep places, which seem almost unable not to
produce a fish, are usually as unprofitable as fishing in a ditch. But
there is a long innocent stretch on the little Exe, for instance, where
a line of great old oaks stretch their branches far out over the
water. And if you can get your line in under there you are almost
always rewarded with a couple of fine fish, usually in remarkably
good condition. I don't know why this should be, except that these
embarrassing oak branches happen to hang over a long stickle, and
the water at that point must be particularly rich with good trout
food. At any rate, fish taken from there are nearly always the best
fish you will get from that mile or so of river. Then, on the Barle,
you can work up a narrow stretch that rushes under a main bridge.
And in here, if you can work your fly properly with the dense
underbrush on either side of you, you will get fish twice the size
you will ever take out of the more likely, broader water lower
down. Those who have fished that bit of water will know the
stretches I am talking about. They will also know the broad stretch
where Exe and Barle meet – to run down into the Black Pool –
where you will hardly ever catch a decent trout.

That's just what makes it all so infuriating, and delectable.
There is a bridge far below with a fine stickle of water running
away from it. By it is an inn. A very modest little inn, where you

know if the sandwiches and bottle of beer in your bag have not been enough, you could always get a hunk of bread and cheese – and some more beer. You may sit there on a bench, tired from the weight of your waders, and have another pint or so before you begin the weary walk home at night; and, as I have said, if you have a half-pound fish to show, then you have caught a whopper.

* * *

I have fished this stretch of water at least three or four Easters . . . usually to repair from the dilapidations caused by too much London. I have fished it in September. And I have watched its flow when there were no fish, when I had come down to that part of the world, for a bit of rough shooting in the late autumn. This was chiefly for cock pheasants. The finest day I remember was a mixed bag of three cock pheasants, one partridge, a black-cock (shot, of all places! in the roots); and a woodcock that I shot in a swampy bottom, going down along a long line of red beeches just as the sun came down.

I have never caught a fish worth talking about, except for the pleasure in catching it. But I know some of the rocks and ledges and stickles in those rivers as well as I know my own door-step. I love that county. I love the life it holds – the bogs, the spinneys; yes, even the almost vertical hills where you slip and slide in the snow of a wintry sunset. I love this English scene.

And I hope that no war, or no such evil thing as 'progress', will ever change it.

From THE ANGLER'S ENGLAND

BY PATRICK CHALMERS (1938)

The char is of the blood royal, is of the *salmonidae*, and he comes from very long ago. He is Arctic in origin, and his colours – his pinks, his greens, his vermilions – have been borrowed from the Northern Lights. And he came – how did he come into the dark tarns and Highland deer forests and the deep places of the bonny land of lakes?

It is said that he came with the push of the icepacks, with the glacier waters of the Age of Ice. And that when the pale blue glacial rivers, the terrible days of the ice-melt, could run no further, some of their waters remained to mingle, here and again, with lakes, tarns, and lochans, in the deep beds that their mother Ice made for them in her final harbour. And therein stayed the char, men say, and there he stays still.

And did ever he come to those cold surfaces to feed on flying-ants and straddle bugs (only he rarely does) he might have seen the great survivors of the Pleistocene come down to drink. The giant fallow, perhaps, walking like an oak tree in his antlers; the cave bear shuffling and mountainous; the sabre-tooth tigress and her two savage golden-coated cubs; the mammoths, grotesque and solemn, who knows what awful else?

But the great brutes went, while the little char stayed and stays still. Listen then.

It was after the Ice Age, but before that of the motor-car. It was July, and it was 6 a.m. when the waking sun walks on all his tiptoes like a golden crab, that two little boys, a bundle of fishing-rods and easel legs, and an elder person with a paint box, packed into a wagonette to drive twenty miles, up from the laigh, into the very shadows of Lochnagar, all to catch little trout, or impressions, in the fastnesses of a deer forest. And adventure indeed.

And the loch, that is in the heart of the forest, is like a black opal to see as it lies, walled and encompassed by cliff and precipice, and flawed by a mystery of little winds and by the blue reflections of heaven. And, when its ramparts of naked rock have done with it and their climb, they cause the summer sky that roofs it to appear from the boat to be more purple than pansies. And it is no fable that has been told concerning the creels of little trout that may be caught here, of the pictures that water-colours may paint.

The loch is nearly a mile long and about a quarter broad but it looks no bigger than a dish, because the hills are so high. And wherever you look, its surface is ringed with rising trout. Their average is a bare quarter of a pound if I remember aright, I, who (it seems more remote than any ice age) was once a little boy, and one of the two anglers. But those small mountain trout fight like tiger-cats and take by twos, sometimes threes, at a time.

The head stalker himself (for the sake of Auld lang syne and of the elder person, who will ashore and be painting) rows the boat. He is old, or he seems to be so to the anglers, but he is the fine man to see, eagle beaked, and splendidly bearded . . .The boat drifts on.

'Is it deep here, Chisholm? Are there big fish here, Chisholm?' inquire the two anglers, suddenly and as one.

Says Chisholm, 'I mind that his lordship was fishing himself at night and a fish took him . . .'

'Oooh, what sort of a fish was it that broke him, Chisholm?'

'God kens, sir, a muckle fish – a fairack maybe!' The boat drifts on. The rise, for the moment is done. Then, suddenly, I am playing another, but? But? The quarter-pounder that comes fighting to the net is scarlet and green and orange – oh surely here is such a capture as never man made before! And yet, 'It's just a bit char,' says Chisholm dispassionately. 'There's ay an odd yin in her.'

There is a pannikin, a bailer, in the boat and, moved by some precious sense of beauty, the angler scoops the same full of the cold, deep, water, enlarges the char in it alive, and desires that the boat may be rowed to the beach that the elder person may at once wonder and mark.

And wonder and mark he does, telling the while of the loveliness and antiquity of chars.

And, 'What are you going to do with it?' he asks. An awkward question that.

'Oh, I dunno; kill it, I suppose.'

'Nonsense,' says the elder person, 'why, you've made a pet of it now, one simply *doesn't* kill pets – far better put the poor little chap back into the loch again.'

So, a trifle, perhaps, in the devotional spirit of David the Kind when he 'coupit' the water of the well of Bethlehem, outboard the bailer is inverted, and, with a kick of colour, the char is gone.

From FISH, FISHING AND THE MEANING OF LIFE

BY JEREMY PAXMAN (1994)

Jeremy Paxman is perhaps best known as the presenter of *Newsnight* and *University Challenge*. He has written two books, *Friends in High Places: Who Runs Britain?* and *The English*, as well as editing *Fish, Fishing and the Meaning of Life* from which the following extract is taken.

The fisherman loves his tackle. It is an obsessive love and, like most obsessions, irrational. Golfers do not, after all, talk fondly about their three irons; footballers don't hurry home after a game to polish up the ball. Yet anglers will spend hours debating the relative merits of rods, reels, lines, bits of metal, plastic, fur and feather which to any impartial passer-by look nearly identical.

None of these obsessives was born obsessional. Something made them that way. My guess is that they wouldn't be obsessional if it weren't for the sheer fickleness of fishing. Every new device which promises – however bogusly – to stack the deck in the angler's favour offers the prospect of success next time. To visit the tackle shop is to enter the temple of enchantments, where each

seductive, plastic-wrapped gizmo suggests there will be no more
Ones That Got Away.

I love these places, with their smell of mothballs, rubber and
waxed cotton. Sometimes, there's a whiff of something more
stomach-churning, usually because someone has bought a stock of
maggots or shrimps and then lost them under the counter. In any
but the most corrupt or inept, you're sure of a warm welcome. It is
the most congenial way to part with your money. Anglers have
been drawn to tackle shops ever since Izaak Walton visited the
Three Trouts in St Paul's churchyard, perhaps the most appropriate
location imaginable for a business dealing in promises.

Yet the staff are no snake-oil salesmen. In the best places they
have the worldly-wise attitude of people who have seen it all
before. This is usually because they have. The eagerness of
fishermen to believe is not seen quite the way a car salesman
watches his mark stroke the shiny bonnet. Being anglers
themselves, the tackle-shop men share the enthusiasm. They would
rather be fishing than working, anyway, and half an hour talking
about the state of the river is better than another £50 in the till.
Admittedly, they have an easy time of it, for the fisherman's
appetite for tackle is unlimited. You have a shoebox full of
spinning lures in red and green and yellow and silver? That doesn't
mean you don't need another. Even another in exactly the same
colour. It's a slightly different size. It swims in a slightly different
way. It's lighter. It's heavier. Above all, it's untested, and therefore
it promises all things. The conundrum of fishing tackle is how
functional objects like hooks or nets or even a bag of purple-dyed
shrimps vacuum-packed in salt can be given an imaginative life of
their own.

No cricketer makes his own bat, but plenty of fishermen make
their own rods. And because all anglers are forever either
modifying their tackle or making it themselves (particularly flies for
salmon and trout), the tackle shop is where you are allowed entry
to the imagination of others, marvelling at how someone else has
noticed that if you tie the wings of a trout fly just a little more
upright, they look so much better from underneath, or that if you

fit a ring to the middle of the net it stops it catching when you climb over barbed-wire fences. It's just the thing. I'll take it.

So it is all the more surprising that fishing tackle took so long to evolve. For most of history, certainly from the time of the ancient Egyptians, anglers fished with their line tied to the top of their rod. Reels, which allowed the angler to control any fish he caught far more effectively than had previously been possible, seem to have become common in Britain during the seventeenth century. They are a pretty simple piece of engineering, giving the opportunity to launch fly or worms into places which would otherwise have been quite out of bounds, so it is surprising that it took three thousand years or so to invent them.

Before that, because the line was attached to the rod tip, if you hooked a big fish the only thing to do was to drop the rod in the water and let the fish wear itself out towing a branch around behind it. Because rods had to be huge, too. The one described in the earliest British fishing book, the *Treatyse of Fysshynge with an Angle* – conventionally and probably wrongly attributed to Dame Juliana Berners, prioress of Sopwell Nunnery, Hertfordshire – describes one twelve feet long. Izaak Walton's collaborator, Charles Cotton, talks of rods of fifteen or eighteen feet: they had to be that length if the fisherman was to be able to get his fly onto the water.

By the time *The Compleat Angler* was published, the first fishing tackle shops had appeared. With them came the first of the interminable discussions about the relative merits of different types of rod. Cotton praises Yorkshire rods, made with butts of fir and six to twelve pieces spliced together, tapering to a fine point. This was usually made of whalebone, the rod itself of hazel or sometimes cane. The line was made from the hairs of a horse's tail, knotted together, again tapering from thick to thin.

By the nineteenth century, with the reel now commonplace, rods were getting shorter. The Caribbean colonies produced a new wood, greenheart, from which mighty great salmon rods were built, stronger and more reliable than previous rods, but exhausting to use. Soon, this too was superseded by split cane, which was lighter, more flexible and therefore more reliable. For fly fishing, lines of greased silk tipped with a gut cast allowed the fly to be floated on the surface of the water. Like most of the breakthroughs in fishing technology, split cane was brought to the highest pitch of refinement in the United States.

Nowadays, most rods are made of fibreglass or carbon fibre – lighter again than split cane and often with a lot more power. They come in all sizes and with all manner of specialist applications. Together with plastic-coated lines which will float, sink, float just under the surface, sink quickly to great depth, and doubtless, in the fullness of time, which will simply do as they're told, the modern fisherman has more choice, more technology and fewer excuses than ever before.

From THE FISHERMAN'S BEDSIDE BOOK

BY 'BB' (1987)

Denys Watkins-Pitchford (1905–90), otherwise known as 'BB', was born in 1905. He wrote books for both adults and children, but his best-known works are those that quickly established him as one of the great British naturalists. In 1937 he published *The Sportsman's Bedside Book* followed a few years later by *Wild Lone: The Story of a Pytchley Fox*. 'BB' also contributed articles to *The Field*, *Country Life* and *Shooting Times*, each of which attest to the rich fund of his experience and his capacity for shrewd observation.

The following extracts are two of my favourites. They show his abiding love of the countryside in the most lucid of prose and are always, to my mind, a great joy to read.

THE BRIDGE

THERE IS A MYSTERY ABOUT A BRIDGE WHICH SPANS ANY WATER; like a magnet it draws the fisherman and the loafer, and the idler is never idle when he is leaning on the rounded coping-stones. These stones are worn as are the steps to some saint's shrine, not by feet but by worshipping elbows of contemplative men and boys and good-for-nothings. Bridges do not seem to attract women – but then, they are not so affected by water nor have they the time to idle.

Few men can pass over a bridge without looking over it, even if they are in a hurry. Even a fishless stream has magic by a bridge. Upon the under-arch bricks the reflected light plays to and fro, like notes of rare music, and from the high vantage-point above one may see the little minnowlings poised in the current and maybe a lusty chub or trout sliding sideways over spotted stones and bright tins. The tins are there because in an effort to break the spell men must drop things into the tawny current and ragged urchins, freed from the scholastic collar, throw stones.

I remember a bridge where I used to linger as a small boy. It spanned a brooklet not ten feet wide, the water held no fish, not even a miller's thumb or stickleback, yet I could not leave that place.

Terrible penalties were threatened if I should ever attempt to wade, but one day I saw a glittering object just under the rose-red arch where ferns sprouted. It gleamed like a blurred pearl down there and as I gazed I knew I must have it, even at the price of a beating.

In I went, treading delicately on small blue feet, revelling in the exquisite first shock of the crinkling stream. And bending there in the gloom of the archway I put my finger into that magic mirror and drew forth an empty mussel shell. To me that pearly spoon was something of great rareness. Clutching it I hastened up the bank, barefooted still and overcome with triumph. And there was Authority sternly eyeing me and a voice came as of thunder. I had disobeyed!

The pearly treasure trove was snatched away and dashed to pieces on a stone, and I was bidden to put on my stockings and boots. This I did with tears coursing down my cheeks and then, in silence far more terrible than scoldings, I was led away and punished.

Another bridge I knew was of wood. It spanned a tributary of the Ouse. Under it the deep water had much mystery and sometimes when the sun shone one could see, deep down among the waving weeds and snake-like ropes of lily roots, vast fish majestically questing, secret fish in a secret kingdom of which they were the finny kings. I have never seen such chub anywhere as those below the sheep bridge – but then the youthful mind magnifies.

And lastly there is the high bridge over a northern river, where the water is so deep that the eye cannot penetrate the gloom. A clear river when not in spate, as most Highland rivers are, under the far-flung arch it had the hue of stout, and in sharp contrast, flat and sculptured rocks were pale and ashy.

Once, gazing down into those inscrutable depths, I beheld a miracle.

Something suddenly became visible, a silvery dimness which, in a moment, resolved itself into a glorious salmon, glittering far more resplendently than my pearl mussel shell. It soared into the air and, curving, hit the water again with a mighty splash which echoed hollowly in the arch. In a second it was gone again and those black deeps had closed over it. I shall never forget that amazing revelation.

A WARWICKSHIRE TROUT

I have never captured a record fish but I have caught two 'notable' fish, one a trout and the other a tench. The trout came out of a brook in Warwickshire where no trout were supposed to be, but I afterwards found out this supposition had been cleverly bruited abroad by those whose lands adjoined the brook. The stream was certainly unprepossessing to the uneducated eye. It was very narrow, much overgrown with bushes and the banks patrolled by bulls. The latter, I have no doubt, had been placed there by riparian owners. But what are such trifles to a small boy? Any active and healthy boy is a match for a bull if he keeps his head and as for keepers and farm bailiffs . . .

When I was about thirteen years of age I went to stay one spring with my grandfather, who, in his day, had been a keen fisherman. He had a coachman named Dickon, who wore a glass eye, always an object of morbid fascination to the young. Dickon had lost his eye one winter afternoon when he was chopping wood, a chip flying up had almost gouged it out.

But I digress. One spring morning I was with Dickon in his harness-room watching him polishing the brass fittings to a collar. I remember that harness-room very well, it smelt of saddle soap, leather, and, of course, Dickon. The combination of all four odours was not unpleasing to my juvenile tastes as I sat swinging my legs on a high stool.

The conversation turned to fishing. 'Ah,' Dickon said, polishing away at a buckle, 'there *are* trout if you knows where to look for 'em. Didn't Mr Free used to get up at five in the morning when he stayed here, and go out and catch them?'

'Trout?' I asked incredulously.

'Aye, trout. Good 'uns too!'

'Where did he go?' I asked.

'Why, Pedder's Mill, of course.'

'But the Commander told me that there were *no* trout there!' I exclaimed. (The Commander being the chief 'riparian owner.')

Dickon smiled and went on polishing. That was enough. I would go to Pedder's Mill as soon as I could get my tackle together.

The next day I developed a roaring cold in the head. But despite this, and managing to conceal my malady from adult eyes, I set off soon after breakfast with my trout rod neatly dodging my grandfather who was talking to Dickon by the coach-house.

It was a wild April morning, grey and blowing hard, with occasional showers. Though the wind was cold it was one of those days when you feel the spring everywhere, you hear it too, and smell it.

I reached Pedder's Mill and had barely rigged up my tackle in the shelter of the hawthorns by the old mill pool (they were speckled over with bursting green buds and a thrush had built a very new emerald nest in the heart of one of them) when the miller up at the mill opened the hatch and the still water at my feet became alive with thundering turmoil, dead leaves appeared and drowned sticks turned over and over in the muddy maelstrom.

Then came the miller and ordered me off. I went out on the road, walked down it for a quarter of a mile and rejoined the brook.

I lay low under a willow stump until I saw the Commander come down the drive in his neat trap, complete with cockaded coachman, and then began to fish. Soon a man appeared up by the Dower House kitchen garden fence, and bawled at me at intervals. I took no notice for a time until he began to purposefully climb the fence. Bailiffs and bulls are best left to themselves. He meant business so I stood not upon the order of my going.

These interruptions were tiresome and this latest interference made me impatient. I made another détour and came upon the stream again. Here, under a palisade of alder trees I at last got my fly on the water and fished the brook down for some two hundred yards without the sign of a rise. Then the stream took a sharp turn to the left in a sort of elbow.

Under the far bank, the current was swift and the fly tittupped round on the ripples and was engulfed. The reel sang as a big fish made upstream and I had to follow. He made for a biggish pool some twenty yards above and there we fought it out for twenty minutes. I had no net (the very young do not carry nets) and I had to play my fish right out and beach him on the shingles at the pool head.

He was a beauty and I took no chance with him, he was practically drowned when I towed him ashore and fell upon him, a trout of three and a half pounds.

The battle won I wrapped it up in dock leaves and put it in my pocket, though the tail flapped under my right arm. I regained the road and almost at once heard the sound of a fast-trotting horse. It was as I had feared, the Commander was returning.

I raised my cap respectfully, and then I heard the clatter of hooves mingle and stop as the trap was pulled up. The Commander was a red-faced man, clean-shaven, of course. He glowered at my rod. I endeavoured to keep my right side turned from him lest he should see the 'tell-tale tail'. I wished the ground would open and engulf me but at that moment Providence took a hand. There came again the sound of trotting hooves and just as the Commander was about to cast aside his carriage rug and descend upon me, no doubt with the object of searching my small person, there swept round the corner my grandfather, likewise in his trap, with Dickon beside him. Under the confusion of the meeting I bolted through a hedge and ran all the way home.

Now, by hook or crook, I had made up my mind to have that fish 'set up'. As bad luck would have it my grandmother met me in the drive and I foolishly showed her my trout, telling her I was going to have it stuffed.

She said nothing, probably because she knew I was a determined young devil, but when my grandfather returned, having calmed the Commander, she told him I was going to have my big trout 'stuffed'.

'That trout will be eaten here,' he thundered, and, as I was afraid of my grandfather, I said no word. Next day I was due to leave for home and without saying anything to anyone I raided the larder, procured my trout and wrapped it up in paper, posting it off from the post office ere I left for the train.

In the queer way grown-ups have, the trout was forgotten in the business of seeing me off to the station and on the way thither I confided in Dickon what I had done, and he gave me unqualified approval. That is why that three-and-a-half-pound brook trout still surveys me as I write these lines, superbly mounted in an ebony framed case, a pleasant reminder of boyhood's triumphant victory over elders and betters, and an aldermanic fish.

From COUNTRY TALES: OLD GILLIES

BY TOM QUINN (1998)

Country Tales: Old Gillies, from which the following extract is taken, is the result of many years' research by Tom Quinn. In it he has gathered together first-hand accounts and recollections from some of Britain's longest serving gillies and, as he says in his Introduction, 'The stories of their lives, are, in part at least, stories of great change. Most obviously fishing tackle has developed out of all recognition during the past fifty or sixty years, from the days of great brass reels and heavy greenheart rods to the ultra-light carbon and boron rods of the 1990s.' Reading the following extract, one can't help but feel that not all change is for the better . . .

* * *

PRINCE CHARLES ONCE DESCRIBED BERNARD ALDRICH, RIVER-keeper on the Broadlands Estate in Hampshire for more than thirty years, as 'a wonderful companion on the river'. The Prince went on to praise Bernard's sense of humour, cheerful personality and commitment to, and deep love for, his river. Bernard Aldrich was born in London, in Woolwich, in 1929 and came from a background with no fishing connection. So how did it all start?

'Well I suppose it was luck really,' explained Bernard when I went down to meet him at the Broadlands fishing hut. 'When I left school I served in the Merchant Navy for a while. I left the Navy to get married and became a policeman, but again this was only for a short time. My sister married a Romsey boy and my wife and I used to come down for holidays. I met my predecessor, Walter Geary, during one of these holidays. He'd been keeper on the river for fifty-two years. I got friendly with him and at this time Lord Mountbatten, who owned the estate, was nagging Walter to get a replacement for when he retired. Old Walter used to say to me, "I don't know what to do. I don't know anyone who could take over." So one day I said to him, "What about me?" We went along after that to see Commander Neill, who was the agent, and I started work. This would have been in 1956. I worked with Walter for five or six years and then he handed the reins to me.

'Long after he'd retired I used to go and get him and bring him down to the river – we were like a big family. Walter knew all those who came to fish and he liked to come down just to be with them and to fish with them.'

Bernard's stretch of the Lower Test was famous for its salmon fishing, but like most of the chalkstream keepers he saw stocks dwindle over the years up to his recent retirement. He was convinced that the river had become dirtier over the years and this pollution together with the pressure of increasing numbers of people also disturbed the wildlife.

'We used to have otters, but as the numbers of people coming down increased they gradually vanished. We disturbed them and they went away. It's very sad. When I first came it was all much wilder. There was no track down to the river. If you wanted to fish you had to walk down or risk driving across a very muddy field.'

For Bernard, work on the river long ago settled into a regular pattern. He started work each day before eight and didn't finish until eight or nine in the evening.

'First thing every morning I went down to our fish farm to clean up and feed the young fish. Then I would wait for the first anglers to arrive. The regulars went straight to the beats where they were booked. If strangers were coming I'd take them down and show them where to fish, and, if necessary, how to fish. Basically I just gave them as much information as I could about the river. Usually it was sons, wives and daughters who came along and needed to be shown how to cast. We had a rota for the fishing and, all told, we had five miles of main river and three miles of trout fishing on the carriers.'

Over the years Bernard taught or assisted a veritable *Who's Who* of famous anglers including Princess Grace of Monaco, Prince Rainier, Admiral Nimitz from the USA and Douglas Fairbanks Junior. But the anglers he remembers most vividly are Prince Charles and Earl Mountbatten.

'Mountbatten only fished during my early days. He was pretty good at it as I recall, but he didn't really have any great enthusiasm for the sport. Prince Charles, on the other hand, had always been very keen. He was taught to fish by his Scottish gillie and by me. He would have been about five when I first knew him and Mountbatten used to bring him down to the river with Princess Anne.

'I can remember one occasion when Mountbatten asked me to find a salmon for the two children to see. I found one under a bridge where there was usually a fish. The problem with fish in this position was that you had to lower the bait to them from the upstream side of the bridge. Then when you hooked the fish you had to let it tear off downstream unhindered. If two people knew

what they were doing, one would hook the fish, let the line fall slack and then drop the rod in the river so that it would drift downstream under the bridge. The angler below the bridge would then pick up the rod. Once fisherman and fish were on the right side

of the bridge it was a relatively easy matter to play the fish.
Everything went according to plan with the two royal children
lying flat on their faces on the bridge, peeping through the bridge
planks down into the water where the fish was lying waiting for the
bait. It was taken by the fish, but the Earl then forgot to let the line
go slack. He held on so tightly that the fish got off. The Prince was
the only one who said anything. He just said, "My daddy wouldn't
have lost the fish."'

After their wedding Prince Charles and Princess Diana came to
Romsey for their honeymoon. As Bernard recalls, this was a time
he found more than a little trying.

'Those damned journalists never stopped pestering us the
whole time the couple were here. We were quite literally under
siege. Reporters arrived twenty-four hours a day. They tried bribing
the staff for information – they tried bribing me. I would have
quite happily shot a few of them. They really were buggers. My
phone used to ring at five in the morning. And they used to ask
such stupid questions like, "Are they enjoying themselves?" I used
to just keep repeating that it was a private visit and it was going to
stay private. I even had a chap from the *Melbourne Times* ring me
up. Mind you the fact that we said nothing made absolutely no
difference. They just made up what they hoped we'd say.'

Bernard had an unusually close relationship with several
members of the Royal Family and has nothing but praise for them:
'They always did their utmost to put people at their ease, but of
course we all get tongue-tied, which is the last thing they want. We
hold them in awe, but I genuinely believe that they don't see
themselves as anything out of the ordinary. Whether it's Prince
Charles or the Queen Mother – who also fished here – they are
always quite happy to follow your suggestions about where and
how to fish. If I used to say try there or over there they would
always do it.'

In his time at Broadlands, Bernard saw many changes and not
just in terms of the increasing sophistication of tackle and
technique. He also charted the immense social changes that took
place during his thirty-five years on the river. In a way the river was

a microcosm of the erosion, in the wider world, of restricting social barriers.

'The changes were perhaps most obvious in terms of dress. People used to come down dressed specifically to fish. They all wore tweeds and I wore a tweed suit and a hat and tie bought specially for me by the estate. I think all that formality began to disappear as younger, more affluent people began to come down to fish. In the old days I wouldn't have dreamed of calling anyone by their Christian name. I was always expected to call everyone "Sir". Towards the end I was on first name terms with about 95 per cent of those who fish at Broadlands, but I still remember that old tweed suit. I used to get a new one every year, complete with plus-fours.'

In those early days Bernard was also expected to take great care of each angler's tackle – down to the last detail. 'There was no nylon when I first came. It was just starting to come in, but it was viewed with great suspicion. Everyone still used catgut. It came in short lengths – each piece was about 1ft long – and it had to be knotted together to make a decent length. It was thick stuff too and very stiff, so you had to damp each piece overnight.

'We had what were called cast dampers – they were like small felt pads. You packed about six casts in these to keep them nice and supple. At lunchtime we'd put the casts into the river to keep them from stiffening. The great thing about gut was that it turned over beautifully when you cast. Ordinary nylon just doesn't turn over properly, that's why people started to use braided nylon for their casts.

'I can remember the old greenheart rods: the Grant Vibration and the Castle Connel. Greenheart had a very slow action and it weighed a ton. Greenheart rods were also spliced. A lot of people today just don't realize how different things were then. The rods had no ferrules – the sections were just lashed together with leather thongs – that was literally all that kept them together. They vanished long before I retired but I thought their demise was sad as they were beautifully made things. Apart from their weight the great problem with greenheart rods was that they dried out badly and one day you'd be fishing and they'd literally explode in a cloud of dust – usually when you were into a good fish. When I first came here I knew every angler's rod and its peculiarities. I'd take them out of the fishing hut ready for whoever I knew was coming to fish. We had a lot to do for each angler then. We'd rub goose fat into the silk line, soak their casts in the river, run their silk lines off the reels and wind them onto wooden line-driers. These were like big wooden reels. At the end of each season each line would be dressed with French chalk to get it through the winter without rotting.

'Although a lot of hard work went out of the riverkeeper's job because of the improvements in fishing tackle, we didn't feel we were a lot better off because there always seemed to be more to do on the river, with bank maintenance, repairing the fishing huts and the bridges. We also had a coarse-fishing lake to look after and although there were three of us, in the very early days there were four, and that was in the days before we had the fish farm and the lake. Keeping the banks in order was always a sod of a job, but it had to be done.'

The trout fishing at Broadlands was always good, but towards the end of his time on the river, Bernard had to stock the river with fish bred on the estate. The salmon situation was more worrying.

'There's no doubt that the salmon fishing just wasn't as good at the end of my time as it had been twenty years earlier. We caught sixty fish in 1988. That's not a large number, but it was a slight improvement on the previous year, which was our worst ever. In that year we caught just thirty-nine fish. The problem, of course, is that we had no control over the high-seas netting industry.'

But if the anglers failed to find as many salmon in the river as they would have liked, they certainly found some strange items over the years. Bernard again:

'We found a mass of strange wooden piles in the river years ago. They were obviously very old and they certainly weren't part of any river maintenance work that had ever been carried out. We contacted someone from the Mary Rose Trust who came and took away some samples of the wood, but we never heard another word about it. Other odd things have turned up in the river from time to time, terrapins, for example. I was gutting a fish one day when what looked like a small turtle suddenly swam up out of the depths of the river and grabbed some bits and pieces floating away from the fish. I managed to catch that terrapin and we put it in his lordship's fountain where it remains to this day.'

The present owner of Broadlands is Lord Romsey, who doesn't fish. Lady Romsey was once very keen and she was taught by Bernard.

Other curious items found in the river over the years include an unexploded 16in shell. This was spotted lying in clear water in the middle of the river and it caused something of a panic. As it turned out the shell wasn't quite what it seemed.

'Yes, we were very worried about that shell so we brought the military in to defuse it or blow it up carefully or whatever. When they got here the whole thing turned into a bit of an embarrassment because the shell was actually just a piece of wood. Mind you, even the bomb disposal people were astonished at how much it looked like a real shell. In fact they were so impressed that they took it away for their museum. It was sheer chance that the wood had been weathered to look like a bomb.'

Bernard still laughs at the memory of the phoney shell and he has many other happy memories from his early days at Broadlands, particularly from the time when he worked with Walter Geary:

'Oh, yes, Walt was a bit of a joker. I remember one very funny trick he pulled on a group of Americans. We used to catch massive, well-mended kelts in the river in February and one day Walter was just in the process of returning a particularly fresh-looking kelt – it was so clean and silver looking that it really did look like a fresh fish. Anyway, a group of Americans nearby asked why he was putting back such a big fish so Walter told them, with a completely straight face, that it was too small to keep. Their mouths dropped open when they heard that, but Walt never let on. They must have gone away thinking that our takeable fish were absolutely gigantic.'

The record for salmon on the Broadlands fishery is recorded in the estate ledgers which detail every fish caught since the 1880s. It weighed 43lb and was caught in 1883. Since that time other massive fish have been hooked – and lost.

'I remember one almighty fish we hooked down at Webb's Pool. It went tearing round for about half an hour and then charged under the bridge. There was nothing we could do to stop it. We were just passing the rod under the bridge when the line caught on part of the stonework and parted. The most extraordinary thing about that fish was that three days later I found the end of my line in the river, tied it to the end of the line on my rod and played the same fish for another twenty minutes before it finally escaped for good. But I can tell you that really was a massive fish.'

The temptations of giant fish mean that Broadlands was also subject to serious poaching. In one incident when Bernard tried to stop a car-load of poachers escaping he was nearly run over:

'I crept down at night and spotted a group of poachers so we phoned the police, but while waiting for the police to arrive I heard a car coming up from the river. I stepped into the road and flashed my torch at the oncoming car thinking it was the police, but the driver accelerated and missed me by inches. In the old days the poachers down here worked alone and they were pretty harmless, but those days had gone by the time I retired. The modern poacher doesn't just take one fish, he takes as many as he can get away with and is quite willing to attack you in the process. I was lucky I suppose – luckier anyway than our gamekeeper. He was shot in the face by poachers and was lucky to survive.'

Despite retirement Bernard Aldrich still lives on the Broadlands estate and with his dogs and regular visits to the river he says he is busier than ever.

From ROD AND LINE

BY ARTHUR RANSOME (1929)

Arthur Ransome (1884–1967) is among those writers whose books, notably *Swallows and Amazons* and *Peter Duck*, have been read and appreciated by countless children over the years. *Rod and Line* (published in 1929) is also a classic, in fact Sir Michael Hordern declares in his diaries that it is 'quite the best fishing book I've read, it's so amusing and yet full of really good advice and well written, the author really appreciates the sort of fishing that poor anglers like myself can only get.'

* * *

AUGUST AND SEPTEMBER ARE THE BEST MONTHS IN THE YEAR FOR carp fishing, and it is pleasant to turn to the carp from such fish as trout and salmon which put a less insistent strain upon the nerves. But not too often. A man who fishes habitually for carp has a strange look in his eyes. I have known and have shaken hands respectfully with the man who caught the biggest carp ever landed in England. He looked as if he had been in heaven and in hell and had nothing to hope from life, though he survived, and after six years caught an eighteen-pounder to set beside the first.

Carp fishing combines enforced placidity with extreme excitement. You may, day after day, for weeks watch your rod fishing on your behalf (for you do not hold it in your hand), and then, at last, you see your float rise and move off and, striking with proper delay, are suddenly connected to the fastest fish that swims. A salmon keeps it up longer, but I doubt if even he has the carp's appalling pace. Trout are slow, dogged creatures in comparison. Further, carp are immensely strong. To hold them safely you need stout gut, but to use stout gut is to throw away most chances of having a carp to hold. There is something terrifying about the fish. To hook a big one is like being jerked out of bed by a grapnel from an aeroplane. Their speed, size and momentum are enhanced, in their effect upon the mind, by the smallness and stillness of the ponds in which they are to be found. The pleasantest such place I know is the lake in front of a tower that Cromwell burnt, a placid pool where frogs spawn in spring, with ancient trees on the still more ancient dam that holds it up. These trees have, during the storms of several centuries, dropped branch after branch into the lake and the bottom there is rich with decaying leaves and a fortress for fish.

You cast out and pray (1) that you may not hook an oak bough, and (2) that if you hook a carp he may neglect the snags on either side of him and give you just a slightly better chance of catching him by burying himself in the water-lilies in the middle of the lake. You cast out, I say. Alas, there is no longer anything to cast for. The lake was drained for its fish during the war, and the men who took them, took even fingerlings, and left nothing alive that they could see. The carp in that lake, however, did not run very large. There were a few big ones killed when it was drained, but nothing of the size I saw at the week-end in a duck-pond that could scarcely have covered two acres. This pond was square and used for washing sheep. There was a little wooded island in it and a sunken willow tree. Its banks were almost without bushes. It was simply a shallow bath-tub of a pond. It had not even water-lilies. It looked as if it had no fish. When I came to the pond side, I believed I had been misled and was consoled by watching a flock of wild Canadian Geese resting beside it. For some minutes they took no notice of me, then, all together twelve or thirteen of them, they raised their long black necks and a moment later, they rose into the air, cleared the hedge, and lifting slowly, flew away. I was still watching them when I heard something like a cartwheel fall into the pond. Huge rings showed, even on the wind-swept surface. I watched for a particularly clumsy diving-bird to come up again. None came, but just as a gleam of sunshine opened the racing clouds, there was another vast splash and a huge pale gold fish rose into the air, shook himself in a cloud of spray, gilded by the sunshine and his own colour in the midst of it, and fell heavily back into the water.

In a few minutes after that, the rods were up and the baits cast out (with the helping wind it was easy to get them well out towards the middle of the pond). The floats were adjusted so as to lie on the surface, held by the resting shot, while the bait with a couple of feet of fine gut lay on the bottom. The placidity of floats so adjusted is like that of anchored ships. Life has left them. They lie dead, on top of the water. They do not drift. There is no feeling that they may be approaching fish. All that can be hoped is that down below, on the mud, a fish is approaching them. The fisherman can do no more. A yard or two of line lies on the ground beside his reel. Until that line is drawn out he must do nothing. He is immobilized, while tremendous events impend. Chained hand and foot, he waits on destiny. And destiny, rumbling here and there, with terrific splashes of golden leviathans, makes havoc of his nerves. He cannot, like the trout fisher, find expression and relief in lengthening his line and casting over a rise. He must steel himself to leave his rod alone and this enforced inaction in the exciting presence of huge fish, visibly splashing, produced a sort of drugged madness in the fisherman. I could not keep my hands still, nor could I reply sanely to questions. A true record of the life of an habitual carp fisher would be a book to set beside De Quincey's *Confessions of an Opium Eater*, a book of taut nerves, of hallucinations, of a hypnotic state (it is possible to stare a float into invisibility) of visions, Japanese in character, of great blunt headed, golden fish, in golden spray, curving in the air under sprays of weeping willow, and then rare moments when this long-drawn-out tautness of expectation is resolved into a frenzy of action. When, at last, I hooked one of these fish, I could not keep in touch with him, though I was using an American multiplying reel with which, on a trout rod, I have kept easily in touch with a salmon. Again and again he won yards of slack and yet, when he was landed he was no glass-case fish, but quite an ordinary carp, which at the end of the day I put back into the pond. For carp fishing, it was a lucky day. Four times the baits were taken by eels, landed amid anathemas, tempered by the thought of next day's breakfast. Four times they were taken by carp. One fish was landed. Twice the carp shot off with such speed that the reel overran, checked and gave him warning. On the fourth occasion one of the monsters made a direct run of thirty yards and then broke me, the fine gut parting above the float. There then occurred an incident that illustrates the uncanny nature of these fish. My float, lying out in the middle of the pond, turned and sailed slowly in again to my very feet, towed by the monster who then in some manner freed himself, thus returning me my tackle with a sardonic invitation to try again. No other fish is capable of putting so fine a point on irony.

To an Old Friend

by Patrick Chalmers, from Green Days and Blue Days

The end draws near again, and very near,
The first few fluttered beech leaves fall and gleam –
Light skirmishes that dog the dying year –
But still I see you down below the weir,
A shadow in the stream.

Here have you lurked since spring – in sportive guise,
Rallied the meadows to young April's rout,
Here first I marked the marvel of your size,
Here wooed you with each fleeting season's flies –
O alderman of trout!

Here, when the madcap cuckoo makes his mock,
And the rathe wild-rose blushed in earliest June,
The day the mayfly hatched above the lock –
You nearly had it, didn't you, old cock,
Save that you stopped too soon?

Here have I watched as the dawn spread high
Hoping in vain the prejudice of pique
That makes you – obviously – reject the fly
Would send you hurtling through the startled fry
To grab a proffered bleak!

Here likewise have my steps at eve been drawn
And, as the moon made way behind the wood,
(The same old moon that watched the hunting Faun)
I've found the lobworm garnered from the lawn
Did just as little good!

And now the end is near; we part a space
You to your mud and I to mine – in town;
May Easter find us at the trysting place
There where the dancing bubbles spin and race
To meet the first March Brown!

From GONE FISHING

BY MICHAEL HORDERN (1995)

Sir Michael Hordern [1911– 95] was not only one of Britain's best
actors, but also one of its most beloved, with roles ranging from
Toad of Toad Hall to Shakespeare's *King Lear* – although one has
the sneaking suspicion that his favourite role was one that involved
a river, a rod and plenty of fish.

* * *

ICAUGHT MY FIRST FISH WHEN I WAS FIVE AND I HAVE OFTEN
thought that had I been allowed to take it home to show my
mother I might never have been infected with a passion for fishing.
It was a tiddler caught with nothing more than a worm on a hook.
My elder brother, Shrimp, all of eleven years old and very
superior, decreed that it must be released back into the water. 'Put
it back, Michael. It's too small.' I obeyed him but I fixed my mind
to go back the next day to catch another and I've been going back
ever since. Hooked!

Something binds me to this sport but, after more than eighty
years, I still don't know exactly what it is; there is the lure of the
riverbank, with its extraordinary variety of wildlife, the taste of the
trout fried on the riverbank with a nub of butter and the twist of
salt that I always carry, or is it simply the pull of the fish one never
quite caught? I don't know, but it has been a devouring passion
which over the years I have very roughly documented in my fishing
diaries. These are thick, old exercise books the first of which was

bought, so it reminds me, at Gillet's Stationers and Printers, Market Street, Brighton, in 1929.

Fishing language is a kind of private language impenetrable to the non-fisherman, laced with exotic names of flies and technical discussions of the characteristics of different streams and pools. My diaries are monuments to long, wet luckless days, the making of a decent fly, the weight of a salmon or trout and, from time to time, the odd remark about a fishing companion. Very long and often boring and I am sure, only of interest to another fisherman, but they do, I believe, sometimes catch something of the joy of fishing – I would almost say an exaltation comparable with the rare moment on stage when it all seems to come together.

This is an entry from my diary for 1935 which should have been written in red ink!

I've caught a salmon! And on the Dart too. The Brownriggs lent us Wild Goose for the week and Shrimp and Dacia and a girlfriend of D's and a man friend of S's and I occupied the cottage for a misty, heavenly week. Major Cook-Hurle kindly gave me a day on his water and on that great day, Wednesday June 12th I got into a salmon in the flats above Eagles Rock. It was the thrill I had been waiting for all these years. My knees knocked and my heart thumped and I felt so ill that for some time I honestly wished I had never hooked it. I could see myself weeping beside a broken cast in ten minutes' time. I knew how I should feel but I gave the fish hell and in about 7 minutes I had my gaff out but he saw it and fled: With the gaff between my teeth, looking and swearing like a pirate, I played him for another 2 or 3 minutes. I wish I could have seen and heard myself.

Then he was on the bank. 'Michael Hordern', I said in a loud voice, 'has killed a salmon.'

I wanted very badly to cry as I used to when I got good fish. I was too thrilled to go on fishing but picked up the fish and hurried back to Dartmeet. I was across the Dart at one place at great risk to life, limb, rod and salmon just for the pleasure of impressing two trippers on the opposite bank. I succeeded. 'Coo,' they said as I went by, 'what is it?' 'Oh,' I said nonchalantly 'a salmon, you know.'

Mrs Cross (who kept the filling station at Dartmeet) embraced me
voluminously and was as pleased as I was. Not the least pleasant
part of it was the 'schloop' noise it made as it fell on the granite
floor of Wild Goose, a noise I had so often hoped to hear . . .

The photographs Mrs Cross took of me, dishevelled,
triumphant and holding my ten-pound catch, unfortunately never
came out but the ones that Dacia took of me the next day did.

Fishing has always been for me something private and being
solitary is a part of the pleasure. I tend to go on my own and talk to
the trout. As an actor it is the most perfect pastime, particularly
when a show is up and running, and a wonderful antidote to the
essential social element of acting, which is all about teamwork. You
have your days free and some of our best theatres are on very good
stretches of water. I often find the odd ally during a rehearsal
period. Tom Stoppard has become an occasional piscatorial
companion since working with him on his first play, Enter a Free
Man in 1968, and Richard Burton always used to show a certain
interest in the water, though I think he mainly enjoyed poaching . . .

Perhaps one of the most memorable and determined anglers
I've known was a woman. Peggy Howard whom I started fishing
with in my late teens. She was mad keen and lived on Dartmoor.
Salmon and sea trout were her catch. We met for the first time late
one night fishing on the Dart. I was on the curve of the river and
she was on the opposite bank. We had fished like this all week but
had never spoken. As usual I was talking to myself as I fished when
I struck up a little song. It may have been 'Rubus the River' or a
piece of opera, I don't remember, but when I stopped she took up
the song where I had left off. A friendship was made and we fished
like this for years but always, in a way, alone. To give you some idea
of what kind of woman she was and how the fishing bug can grab
one, I recorded this in my diary:

Dart August 1938
Peggy just told me the most terrible fishing story ever. She hooked a
salmon at dusk, as I did, with her Peal rod. It got the wrong side of the
big rock in the middle of the pool and in order to free it she swam rod

and all in the dark to the rock. She freed the fish which then went down
to the tail of the pool. To keep on terms with it, she again swam down to
the tail and twisted her ankle badly in the rocks but continued to play it
sitting on a stone. When the fish was dead beat she saw that the cast was
twisted round and round its head and before landing it she decided, I
can't quite think why, that this must be unwound. This she did only to
discover too late that the salmon wasn't hooked at all and all that held it
was the cast round its gill, once free of the line, the fish floated away out
of her reach.

She returned the next morning to retrieve some line she'd left on the
bank and was amazed to see in the shallow water her salmon drifting
away 'dead'. So she grasped it around the tail, lifted it from the water
but it gave an almighty flip and was gone for good! . . .

I know what inspires me to write this diary: I don't want all
those experiences, all that pain and pleasure, to go unrecorded.
Even if I am the only one who ever reads my diary, I just want to
get it down, to capture the immediacy of the experience. I want to
be able to relive the excitement of the act of fishing; to prevent the
experience being lost or transformed by any uncertain memory. It
is that sense of what it is to fish that I look for in books about
fishing. Abstract discussion of the theory of fishing is not, to my
mind, 'real' writing on fishing.

This is what I find in the limpid poetry of Ted Hughes, the
lively wit of Arthur Ransome, and the sense of personal struggle
that pervades Hemingway's description of his battles with fish . . .

The moment of catching a fish unites all lovers of fishing in the
same, but perhaps ultimately indescribable, joy. I certainly cannot
do it and I admire writers who can and who can evoke the lesser
but profound pleasures associated with fishing, such as watching
the river wildlife.

There are some things I feel one ought to be able to do while
fishing but simply can't. I have tried to learn my lines or resolve
the meaning of life but I find I cannot do it.

Ted Hughes, an avid fisherman, composed a poem for me about
a day when he and I and a few friends went fishing in unpropitious

circumstances. There was snow still on the bank and the season was just opening and though I did not expect that we would catch anything, I thought it would be quite an enjoyable cast. Most of the day had passed when suddenly, Ted felt a fish and, handing me the rod, insisted I land it. So I cast out my fly and started to play the fish. There wasn't much playing to be done. It soared about in the water a bit and I played to my audience of five when I realized it was absolutely dead as a doornail. No one came to my rescue so I waded out with my net, brought it ashore, to find it was not only dead, but frozen rock-solid! They had got it out of the freezer and somehow hooked it on to my line when I wasn't looking!

Ted's poem is a very long spoof epic, depicting a Herculean battle of wills. The fishing party is transformed into the cast of *King Lear*, Ted modestly playing The Fool with a demented laugh. Two of the verses go:

> *And so these shadows of the stage*
> *That God could hardly see*
> *Shattered the ice and waded deeper*
> *Into tragedy,*
> *Like Herons in an afterlife*
> *Where not a fish could be.*
>
> *Till suddenly, 'I've got a fish!'*
> *The Fool let out a screech.*
> *Lear, like the old man of the sea*
> *Came staggering up the beach.*
> *'It's absolutely fresh!' he gasped*
> *'O my God, what a peach!'*

and it ends:

> *Now let us praise the flies of the creator*
> *And such a fly that brought up such a fish*
> *Straight to the Fisher's wish*
> *Out of the depths of a refrigerator.*

I am very proud of it and have it – the poem, not the fish – framed on my wall.

More seriously, my favourite Hughes poem is 'The Pike', in which he succeeds in making me 'see' the fish and it is my favourite fishing poem. However, my favourite fish being the trout, I particularly love Wordsworth's description of the 'bold brook' in 'The Excursion':

> On whose capricious surface is outspread
> Large store of gleaming crimson-spotted trouts;
> Ranged side by side, in regular ascent.

With the start of each new season, I watch the weather closely. I still manage to go out on the Lambourne, occasionally with my brother Shrimp. Sixty years on, he's still a better fisherman than me. We both still have that 'want' to bring the fish home, stumbling and shouting at each other across the bank. I think of the fish as my noble enemy and I want him for my supper. Particularly if it is trout. It is both a fight and a dance and there is always the one that got away.

I am very fortunate: my cottage overlooks the Lambourne in a beautiful part of Berkshire and I have fished for near eighty years. It is a passion that has never loosened its grip on me and one I hope to pass on to my grandson, Nicholas. I read my diaries from time to time, but I must confess that I haven't added to it in recent years. Somehow, the detail is still interesting to me from long ago fishing victories: the pleasure that it was a ten-pound salmon and not the nine-pound I thought I remembered it to be. The diaries have decided many a dispute and, though no literary masterpiece, they plot an idyllic fishing career. In *Coming up for Air*, Orwell writes: 'There isn't a cowpond or backwater that I can't see a picture of if I shut my eyes and think.' This is also true of me.

From REFLECTIONS ON THE WATER

BY FRED J. TAYLOR (1982)

Fred J. Taylor has been a lifelong follower of country pursuits and his knowledge of angling is hard to beat. He has had numerous encounters with such fishy species as roach, bream, eel, carp, trout and salmon, not to mention the American largemouth bass, pike, glow-worms and tadpoles! But as the following extract illustrates, his underlying theme has always been that fishing should be fun and if it *does* cease to be a pleasure, then what is the point of carrying on?

LIGHT RELIEF

There's a great deal to be said for the occasional, light-hearted fishing session that involves no serious preparation and very little in the way of special bait. Throughout the summer months a great deal of our fishing time is spent during the early-morning or late-evening hours trying to catch fish that are often far from co-operative. Most of us agree, however, that the chances then are greater than during the day and we stick at it religiously until we achieve what we want – or until we suddenly realize we're no longer enjoying it.

This ceaseless quest for big fish, special fish (every angler has a particular ambition, I'm sure) can be very wearing if results are not forthcoming. And it's then that a little light relief is called for. It's good for the morale if for nothing else to call a halt to these bloody-minded sessions and to go out and catch something easy – or at least easier.

It doesn't matter really what species are involved. What *is* important is that the fish are free biters and that they do not call for the dawn or dusk approach.

Recently my own light relief (and I welcomed it after a particularly unrewarding bream stint) came in the shape of a

couple of dozen rudd. They were not big – the best weighed only
eleven ounces, but they were *fun* to catch.

Rudd, of course, are not put off by warm water conditions as a
rule, and carp anglers fishing with floating crust during the day
regard them as out-and-out pests, but everything is relative in
fishing. If you want carp on the bank you don't need rudd to
distract you, but if you set out to catch rudd on appropriate tackle
it's a different cup of tea.

Rudd fishing can hold almost as much frustration at times as
some of the more demanding kinds, but usually there's enough
going on to keep you occupied. You can often see activity near the
surface and that's enough to keep you pegging away.

You need tackle that isn't going to be too hard on small fish,
but it has to be good casting tackle because, almost invariably,
feeding rudd tend to drift further away from the bank with every
cast you make.

I had my fun with a little wand of a rod, weighing under two
ounces. My line was 2-pound test, and by using a heavy zoomer-
type float I was able to get a fair distance. This little 'Bo-peep' rod
(my name for it incidentally, not a trade name) isn't designed for
long casting. It's just a one-piece, five-foot, very soft-actioned stick
that bends to the pull of a small fish, and I find it really alarming
when something bigger takes hold. But it's a rod I can use all day
without fatigue and which gives me the maximum pleasure from
small, easy fish.

A number of my friends laugh and say that it's quite
impracticable, that there's no way you can control the line with a
five-foot rod and that a much longer rod would be a more efficient
tool. In many circumstances they'd be right, of course, but for
long-distance shallow fishing for rudd, there's no advantage at all in
a long rod. I would be casting, at times, in the region of forty
yards, with my bait no more than a foot below the surface. Bites
were slow, steady and determined and I could handle them
perfectly well with the short rod. Had I been fishing deep, had the
bites been mere flickers on the float, I'd probably have needed the
extra sweep of a longer rod, but in this particular situation I was

better off with the one I was using. Tucked under a tree as I was, I could not have executed a punch cast with a long rod without fouling the branches above, and these small rudd could never have given me so much sport.

It's a long time since I did any of this long-distance bank fishing for rudd. Most times I drift around for them in the boat, but I am reminded of earlier years when this kind of fishing was common practice. And I am very conscious of the fact that my modern floats are not a patch on those old ones I used fifteen or twenty years ago, which were dart-flight floats that cast well and remained visible at very long range. The thin vanes above the water line offered no resistance to biting fish but they stood out like brightly coloured 'bobbers' against the skyline. The thin-stemmed floats I used the other day were much more difficult to see.

There's still a lot to be said for some of the old ideas, and many of the rigs thought up years ago are still very practical today. I suppose the self-cocking float-cum-floating-crust-groundbait idea for rudd goes back for hundreds of years but it's still very effective today if you can put it to work.

The Victorian anglers used to anchor their floating crust attractors in hairnets so that the rudd remained within casting range, and I've no doubt that the same idea would work today. As it is, most of us, myself included, tend to chuck out a few loose crusts for the rudd to locate, without paying too much attention to their line of drift. The usual result is that the fish eventually drift out of range with the crusts.

But, forgetting the effects of attractor crusts for a moment, it seems to me that, on some waters at least, rudd have a tendency to hug one particular line so far from the bank during the day. They may or may not be wise to anglers' bank shadows, but I've noticed that the better-quality rudd tend to stay well out until evening time. Casting directly to them, dropping a float in their midst, causes them to drift out even further, despite the fact that they'll take the hookbait the moment it lands. It's rather puzzling because this eagerness to take the bait surely proves that they're not actually scared by the tackle's entry. But you can almost be sure that the

next cast you make will
need another couple of feet
added to it.

When I fished the
other day I was fortunate
in that the breeze was
blowing across a wide corner
and not out to the middle of the lake. It made the fishing a lot
easier because, once the fish had drifted out past my maximum
casting range from one bank spot, they just about came into range
from the one opposite. Logically, the fish should have followed the
loose crusts right into the margins where I could have fished for
them under the rod tip, but they would only travel so far before
taking up their original lies.

I spent a great deal of time moving from spot A to spot B in
order to intercept them, and I didn't always succeed, but that's
what made it all the more interesting. Here I had fish willing – even
eager – to bite, and all I had to do was put the bait amongst them.
Not quite as easy as it sounds but a good exercise nevertheless.

It gave me a pleasant afternoon's sport, a nice net of fish plus a
few little problems; and it was a most welcome change from the
flogging I'd been doing.

There are many other forms of what I call 'light-relief fishing'
and I tend to practise them on and off throughout the season when

the going's been tough.

I'll switch from barbel to dace for a time, or I'll leave the carp alone and fish up a storm with the comical little crucians. Sometimes I'll fish for eels during the heat of the day when the tench, bream or carp are off. And every so often I'll take the little 'Bo-peep' and flick out a little jig spinner for pike. I hope I never hook a big one on that outfit because even four-pounders feel like ocean-run monsters! But that's the whole point. I'm not out to break records or prove anything. I'm just seeking relief from a fishing that's become more of a chore than a pleasure.

I reckon everyone performs better after a break from monotony and I truly believe my light-relief fishing helps me handle the serious side a little better.

THE HOOK-SHEDDERS

The day was warm and overcast. My brother Ken and I were walking slowly upstream on opposite banks of the narrow river trying to locate fish for each other, as we often do, but had had very little success so far.

I think we both spotted the big brown together and we stopped dead in our tracks. The fish was holding steadily in the current above a bare patch of gravel and, as we watched, it dived nose first into the patch and began digging into the bottom. After a few seconds it retired to its holding place, remained there briefly and then repeated the procedure, releasing clouds of silty sand as it did so.

'That,' said Ken, 'is the first time I've ever seen a trout feeding like a carp!' And I agreed. It was strange behaviour for a trout and, as its diggings appeared to become more and more frantic as time went by, we tried to figure out what was so special about that particular gravel patch. We cast over the fish several times while it rested at mid-water level, but it showed no interest whatsoever in anything we were able to offer, and we were puzzled. Finally it dawned upon us that this fish was not feeding at all. It was trying desperately to rid itself of a small fly and a length of nylon leader by rubbing its mouth on the hard bottom. It was persistent, I'll say that for it, and we both spent a long time watching it (I nearly said 'wasted a lot of time', but that would have been wrong), almost willing it to succeed.

It was probably an hour before it gave up trying and set out on a long and almost desperate run upstream. It was obviously irritated, though not seriously distressed, but as it cruised up and down between the two bridges it seemed to transfer its irritation to several other hitherto unseen trout causing them to leave their lies and behave in a similar fashion.

For a time, great bow waves showed here and there as fish after fish, thoroughly unsettled, made runs up and down the beat before quietly returning to shelter. It didn't improve the fishing but it certainly served to illustrate how one disturbed fish can affect the behaviour of others.

Several times after that, we spotted the big brown still scraping away at the gravel patch and towards late afternoon we located it again, quiet and finally rid of the hook that had been causing all the trouble. There was a raw spot on its lower jaw where it had obviously rubbed away part of the gristle in the process. Amazingly enough, it began to feed about an hour afterwards, but we weren't smart enough to catch it then, and in a way I was rather glad – I reckoned it deserved a break.

I really find it hard to understand why some anglers persist in fishing for big trout in the confines of a narrow overgrown river with tackle that is obviously inadequate. These fish have to be held hard and there's no way you can hold a big trout on a 2-pound point in these circumstances. Some argue that it is the only way to induce a rise or to fool a fish into taking, but I have never found it necessary to fish finer than 4-pound there. I've lost fish, it's true, but I can honestly say that I do not recall such a loss ever being through line breakage.

I've had hooks pull out and I've had them straighten. I've had the odd one or two break at the barb because I've allowed them to become rusty by sticking them into a wet hat and forgetting them, but I've no recollection of leaving hooks and lengths of nylon in the fish of that water. In trees, yes, many times – but not in fish.

Leaving aside the emotional aspect of what it does to the fish itself, I think it's worth bearing in mind what effect a lost fish can have on other people's fishing. Fish that might otherwise be free feeders become restless and neurotic when another, obviously disturbed fish passes among them, and they'll only calm down in their own good time. There's no way you can make them forget or revert to normal behaviour.

The disturbance is, of course, only temporary and I'd hazard that in a couple of days most fish are able to rid themselves of hooks. I've heard tell of fish being caught with several flies already in their mouths, but I haven't seen it myself, and I can only assume that some hooks or flies embed themselves in spots that do not irritate or inconvenience their 'hosts'.

When you consider the number of fish that are lost all over the country – and I'm including coarse fish here, of course – it's quite astonishing how few of us ever catch fish carrying hooks. I've caught pike with snaps and trebles in them as well as small hooks obviously intended for roach, but with few exceptions they did not give the appearance of having been hooked for long. It's my belief that most fish are remarkably capable of ridding themselves of hooks, but I haven't the faintest idea how it's done.

There was a time when I used to worry about removing the hooks from a badly hooked pike but now I treat each situation as an individual case, and I'm convinced that there are times when it's better to return a fish with the hooks still in. Sometimes, in spite of great care and proper equipment, a pike that undergoes a lengthy, bankside, hook-removal operation is worse off than one that's returned quickly with the hooks trimmed down and left inside.

I'll never forget the story Ian Howcroft told many years ago about the pike he 'killed' and took home because it was too badly hooked to return. Despite a knock on the head and a long journey, the fish was still alive when he arrived and so he put it in the bath and left it to take its chance.

It revived and began swimming around shortly afterwards and

a few hours later both the trebles and wire trace were no longer in its throat but wrapped around the bath plug chain! I've always felt it a great pity that the whole operation wasn't filmed for posterity.

Back in the 1950s I hooked a carp on a soft-boiled potato and a No. 6 treble, and because all points were well embedded deep at the back of its throat I bit the line through and put the fish in a big keepnet. It was pitch dark and I thought I'd do the fish less harm if I worked on it by daylight. At the crack of dawn I took the fish out of the net, intending to remove the hook, but it was no longer there. It was not in the keepnet either, and there were no red marks or signs on the fish of it ever having been there. And unless someone else sneaked along and swapped my fish for another sixteen-pounder, I cannot think what happened to that hook. I can only assume the fish somehow managed to remove it and swallow it along with the foot or so of 11-pound nylon to which it was attached!

It is said that both chub and tench are capable of transferring hooks to weed and rush stems while still attached to a rod and line, but while I *have* occasionally ended up playing a lily stem I can't convince myself that the changeover was intentional!

Some say that a chub can fill its mouth with weed to such an extent that the hook is forced out, but whenever I've hooked a fish, chub, tench, carp, or whatever, in soft weed I've usually found they've given up trying almost at once and that a steady pressure brings them (and half the weed-bed too) into the bank. Occasionally the pressure applied is such that the hook pulls free, and there *have* been times when I've thought the fish was still there but found it very much missing when the weed reached the net. I'm of the opinion, however, that a fish buried in soft weed is capable of doing precious little to help itself, and there have been times when I've been glad to see a big trout bury itself in soft weed upstream – fish that I've been fairly sure I'd have lost otherwise.

Ted Andrews was telling me recently that he hooked a Stour roach of about twelve ounces in the gristly part of the jaw and that he simply could not get it out. To save time he put the fish in the keepnet and tied on a fresh hook in order to make the best of the last half-hour or so while the fish were 'on'. When the time came to release the roach, the hook had disappeared completely.

Here is a case where there was no available leverage and no facilities for a direct pull or tangle, and yet the hook had somehow or other been shifted.

Is it done by muscle contraction or by magic? Perhaps we'll never know, but it's something to puzzle over, and it might help ease our consciences when we lose the odd fish through line breakage.

By the way, Ken caught the trout a week later. It was fat and full of fight and, apart from a raw lip, none the worse for having been hooked.

THE FISH

BY RUPERT BROOKE

In a cool curving world he lies
And ripples with dark ecstasies.
The kind luxurious lapse and steal
Shapes all his universe to feel
And know and be; the clinging stream
Closes his memory, glooms his dream,
Who lips the roots o' the shore, and glides
Superb on unreturning tides.
Those silent waters weave for him
A fluctuant mutable world and dim,
Where wavering masses bulge and gape
Mysterious and shape to shape
Dies momently through whorl and hollow,
And form and line and solid follow
Solid and line and form to dream
Fantastic down the eternal stream;
An obscure world, a shifting world,
Bulbous, or pulled to thin, or curled,
Or serpentine, or driving arrows,

Or serene slidings, or March narrows.
There slipping wave and shore are one,
And weed and mud. No ray of sun,
But glow to glow fades down the deep
(As dream to unknown dream in sleep);
Shaken translucency illumes
The hyaline of drifting glooms;
The strange soft-handed depth subdues
Drowned colour there, but black to hues,
As death to living, decomposes –
Red darkness of the heart of roses,
Blue brilliant from dead starless skies,
And gold that lies behind the eyes,
The unknown unnameable sightless white
That is the essential flame of night,
Lustreless purple, hooded green,
The myriad hues that lie between
Darkness and darkness! . . .

* * *

And all's one,
Gentle, embracing, quiet, dun,
The world he rests in, world he knows,
Perpetual curving. Only – grows
An eddy in that ordered falling,
A knowledge from the gloom, a calling
Weed in the wave, gleam in the mud –
The dark fire leaps along his blood;
Dateless and deathless, blind and still,
The intricate impulse works its will;
His woven world drops back; and he,
Sans providence, sans memory,
Unconscious and directly driven,
Fades to some dank sufficient heaven.

* * *

O world of lips, O world of laughter,
Where hope is fleet and thought flies after,
Of lights in the clear night, of cries
That drift along the wave and rise
Thin to the glittering stars above,
You know the hands, the eyes of love!
The strife of limbs, the sightless clinging,
The infinite distance, and the singing,
Blown by the wind, a flame of sound,
The gleam, the flowers, and vast around
The horizon, and the heights above –
You know the sigh, the song of love!

* * *

But there the night is close, and there
Darkness is cold and strange and bare;
And the secret deeps are whisperless;
And rhythm is all deliciousness;
And joy is in the throbbing tide,
Whose intricate fingers beat and glide
In felt bewildering harmonies
Of trembling touch; and music is
The exquisite knocking of the blood.
Space is no more, under the mud;
His bliss is older than the sun.
Silent and straight the waters run.
The lights, the cries, the willows dim,
And the dark tide are one with him.

CONFESSIONS OF A RANK AMATEUR

BY TOBY BUCHAN (1994)

The following story by Toby Buchan should perhaps be read as an antidote to Jeremy Paxman's observation that all fishermen are obsessed with tackle. No one could accuse Buchan of being this way; in fact he is just the reverse . . .

* * *

GREENWELL'S GLORY. JOCK SCOTT. TUP'S INDISPENSABLE. Black Spider. Thunder and Lightning. Peter Ross. Alexandra. Teal, Blue and Silver. Coch-y-Bonddhu. Iron Blue Dun. Butcher.

The names of some of the great flies echo down the long history of fly-fishing like the roll-call of the ancient heroes. As it happens, these are the names of just about the only flies I can recognize with any confidence.

I don't know why this should be. Like most fishermen, I have fly-books stuffed with patterns of every type and size and description. I must have known the names once, when I bought them, or tied them, or was given them. But then it all goes, and someone will ask me to lend them a Garry, say, and I am forced to bluff, offering the fly-book (secretly hoping it's the right fly-book) and telling them to help themselves. I am the same about hook sizes, and the breaking-strain of nylon, and line weights and tapers, and even rod lengths. A conversation with my brother, who is as shamefully ignorant and forgetful as I am, will go something like this:

'What did that fish take?'

'The Green Job.'

'Oh right – have I got one here?' (Extending fly-book.)

'I think it's that one . . .' (Long silence as the fly is changed.)

'What strength cast are you using?'

'Thinnish.' (This is stronger than thin, but not so strong as thickish, let alone thick.)

Another long silence. Nothing is caught.

'Change the size of fly, d'you think?'

'Mmmm, p'raps. What size?'

'Smallish, prob'ly.' (This, of course, is bigger than tiny and small, but smaller than biggish and much smaller than big.)

Or on another day:

'That's a nice rod. How long is it?'

''Bout nine foot, I think.'

'Is it carbon-fibre?'

'Yup – at least, I think so.'

'What line does it take?'

'No idea – prob'ly says on it, somewhere. I'm going to put on a green one. Is that sinking, would you say?'

'Haven't a clue – see if it sinks, why not?'

So it goes on – defeated by AFTM numbers, tapers, fast, slow, or intermediate lines, hook sizes, cast strengths, above all, by the names of flies and lures, we blunder on along the path of our fishing, fighting our private battles with the tyranny, the anarchic chaos of nomenclature. And as fly-fishing becomes more technical, more specialized, more equipment-based, I find myself increasingly stranded upon the atoll of my own incompetence. Shameful, I know, and doubtless I catch fewer fish than those experts who are always telling me that they just 'Tied a size 18 Pale Watery Dun to

a length of 6X I happened to have, and dropped it on his nose – took me 20 minutes to land him . . .' All of which is largely gibberish to me, and fluent gibberish therewith. What is doubly shameful, however, is that out of a desire not to have my ignorance discovered, I am always giving people duff information.

Not intentionally, of course – I just simply cannot remember.

I caught a biggish (possibly even a big) trout the other day. As I

came off the water, another fisherman
asked me what I'd taken it on. Now had
I been truthful, I should have answered:
'The Orange Job with a bit of gold wire
on it; smallish; got a long hook
something like a Mayfly hook.'

Not wishing thus to show my
ignorance, I lied. 'Woodcock-and-
Orange,' I said, that being the only
orangey sort of fly I could think of on
the spur of the moment. He looked a
trifle startled, but went off quite
merrily. I felt rather guilty about it, to
be honest. Presumably he'd asked because he thought another fish
might take the same pattern. I slunk home, with images of him
spending the rest of the afternoon lashing the surface to a soufflé
with teams of Woodcock-and-Oranges.

Many years ago, I went with a friend – known as The Major,
largely because he is one – to fish Grafham. Used to loch and
lough, we were intensely curious to know what it was like to fish
these huge English reservoirs from which, we had heard, monster
trout in very large numbers were to be caught. We set forth with
our little cane Hardy rods, our little Lock hats set squarely on our
heads, carrying our little Brady trout-bags, our collapsible Sharpe's
nets, our olive-drab thornproofs (then a rarity, rather than, as now,
urban man's fashion accessory).

We noted with amused – I'm sorry to say, perhaps rather
superior – wonder the contents of other boats: the many highly
coloured glass-fibre rods, of enormous length, laid reverently in the
bows; the huge plastic tackle boxes; the well-padded folding seats;
the lines of gay reds or light blues or oranges; the extraordinary
giant flies, looking as though they had come from some favourite, if
eccentric, Edwardian aunt's best bonnet. Sitting fore and aft in our
boat, we cast-and-retrieved our teams of traditional wet-flies,
fishing off the points, hanging off inlets and outlets, working drift
and wind-slick, as we had learned on loch and lough. And as we

did so, we remarked humorously – if, I'm ashamed to say, slightly
snobbishly – on the behaviour in the other boats: Great Heavens,
people were standing up, were casting enormous lengths of line,
were retrieving with astonishing speed.

Pride goeth before destruction, and all that.

When the sun set, we took the boat back, fishless. All around
us other boats were coming in, the only difference being that, after
landing, each began to do a passable reconstruction of the
Miraculous Draught of Fishes.

As we walked back in the twilight, frustrated and a good deal
humbled, we watched another boat land. From it the occupants set
about removing rods, boxes, nets, bags, flasks, and . . . trout. Not
just a few trout, either – the business resembled the unloading of a
newly docked trawler in the days before quotas. We approached
the two fishermen, who, it must be said, exuded the air of men
who have done a job well, and know it. Good show, we said. Well
done. Splendid. Do any good yourselves? they asked. No, we said.
Buzzers, they said. The Major and I looked at each other, if not
with a wild surmise, then at least with one that was a good distance
from being wholly tame. Eh? we said.

You want buzzers, they said. Lash one to a very long cast – like
18 feet long – grease said cast to within an inch of the tip (or
possibly to within an inch of its life; I didn't quite follow this bit),
cobble the whole shebang to a floating line, cast out, and wait to
become ankle deep in trout. Ah, we said, brilliant. Buzzers – of
course. Stupid of us. Must try it. Thanks awfully. Then, torn by
visions either of some sort of doorbell, or of bumblebee drones
with laryngitis, one of us asked, with profound embarrassment, what
a buzzer actually was. Well, they said, ever-helpful and courteous, a
buzzer is a chironomid. At this the Major brightened perceptibly.
Oh, yes, he said, we had one of those, but the wheels fell off . . .

It was not a bad lesson to learn, and to this day I have never so
much as lifted the merest corner of an eyebrow at anyone's tackle,
or kit, or preferred method of fishing. We got the hang of
Grafham in the end, and one day at lunchtime I unloaded a six-
and-a-half-pound brown trout on the jetty. A chap approached

admiringly, and asked me what I'd caught it on. Panic – I knew it was a black fly, but the devil if I knew its name.

'Black Spider,' I said, and off he went, searching excitedly through his fly-book.

That evening, as I prepared to leave, a hand smote me on the shoulder from behind. I turned, to find my friend of the morning.

'How did you get on?' I said, not without trepidation.

'Best tip anyone ever give me, mate – I've got me limit. Ta – yerra sport . . .'

I wonder if his Black Spider and mine are the same thing?

From TROUT BUM

BY JOHN GIERACH (1986)

I love this extract from *Trout Bum* by the American author and fisherman John Gierach. Not only does it sum up what a few other contributors to this anthology have already said, but it does so in such a dry, humorous fashion and, as it goes along, paints a wonderful picture of a man fairly rattling and clanking with 'stuff'!

* * *

I took up fly-fishing long enough ago that I don't remember exactly when it was, but I remember I had the novice's ready-made fascination with all the mysterious gear and gadgets. In fact, it was probably the exotic tackle and accoutrements that first attracted me to the sport. I had previously fished with what I now think of as 'nonfly' tackle, but the stuff fly-fishermen carried was both beautiful and serious looking at the same time – like a big, jangling ring of keys to a different reality. I was clearly hooked on the ambience before I even got started, which is *why* I got started in the first place.

Of course, like all such things, it was more complicated than I

first imagined. I remember walking into a store and announcing
that I'd come to buy a fly rod.

'What kind?' asked the guy behind the counter.

'You mean there are different kinds?'

I asked for a regular-old, garden-variety fly rod and ended up
with a fibreglass seven-and-a-half footer for a # 6 line fitted with a
Pflueger Medallist reel. I passed up the one you could convert to a
spinning rod by doing some fancy footwork with the reel seat.
After all, I was a purist.

It took me a few trips to the store and a bit more money than
I'd planned on – an ominous sign of things to come – but soon I
had what I then considered to be the full getup: a small,
inexpensive, flimsy vest, some leader material, a bottle of mosquito
repellent, a pair of Taiwanese ditchboots, and a box of about a
dozen flies, also from somewhere in the Third World. The flies
were nice and big and real pretty.

At first I thought I was in business, but it wasn't long before I
started feeling half naked next to the archetypal properly attired
fly-fishermen I'd meet on the streams. Some of these guys were
pretty impressive; they looked like combinations of tackle stores,
biology labs, and hospital emergency wards. The rattling, clanking
sound they made when they walked had an authoritative ring to it,
and most of them seemed to have evolved elaborate personal
systems for balancing a strung-up fly rod, fly box, forceps,
micrometer (you can't trust factory measurements on this tippet
material, you know), imported English scissor/pliers, etc.

They'd descend on the stream like information-gathering
modules, sprouting collection nets, specimen bottles, and stream
thermometers, and could often be heard muttering to each other in
some foreign language I later discovered to be Latin: 'Clearly one of
the large, Ephemerella, probably the doddsi, though possibly the
glacialis, easily mistaken for the E. grandis. Better tie on an Adams.'

The only Latin I could remember from college was *cogito ergo
sum* ('I think, therefore I am'), I think.

The clincher was that most of these guys seemed to catch more
trout than I did, and the only obvious difference between us was

all that equipment. I began to suffer from voidophobia – the unreasoning fear of empty vest pockets. I didn't know exactly what I needed, but I clearly needed a lot of stuff, enough stuff to make me clank and rattle when I walked, to strain the single-stitched seams of my cheap vest, enough to put me in the same league with the guys who were catching all the fish.

By this time I'd figured out there were shops that dealt exclusively in fly tackle. (I'd bought my first gear at a place that also sold tires, garden tools, school supplies, Mexican felt paintings, and hot dogs.) I've since worked in fly shops and have cringed to see myself in some of the rosy-cheeked types who came in and asked things like, 'What size fly do I need to catch a 20-inch brown?' or 'How do I tie this little bitty fly to this big fat fly line?'

'Well . . . you need a leader.'

'A what?'

A clerk in the average shop spends half his time patiently leading people from the middle back to somewhere near the beginning.

Luckily, I happened to walk into the now-defunct Hank Roberts shop on Walnut Street in Boulder, Colorado. Had I stumbled into the clutches of an unscrupulous tackle dealer, I could easily have been fleeced of my life savings, such as they were. I wanted *stuff*, lots of it.

As it was, I was sold a few flies (Adamses and Hare's Ears), a tapered leader and some tippet

material, and one of those fancy double-tapered lines to replace my
level 6. I was even treated to a free casting lesson out in the parking
lot.

'Look, you're not throwing a rock, you're casting a fly rod. Let
the rod do the work.'

'Yeah, right, oof, oof, oof.'

'And by the way, when you get a chance, you might want to get
yourself a *decent* rod.'

There were some decent rods back inside, rods with names like
Leonard, Thomas & Thomas, and Orvis on them. A few cost more
than the pickup truck I was driving, some of the gray smoke from
which was still drifting through the open front door. Some of them
were made from some kind of blonde-colored wood that was
sawed up into six strips.

'Split cane.'

'Huh?'

'Bamboo.'

'Oh, right, I had a bamboo rod when I was a kid.'

'(sigh)'

I didn't know it then, but I'd been treated well. Still, I was
disappointed that I didn't clank and rattle any more than I did
before, and after spending a fair piece of change, too.

I started reading magazines, and then books on the subject.
There was this guy named Ernest something (not Hemingway) who
seemed to know a lot about bugs. Well and good, but what size fly
do I need to catch a 20-inch brown?

Slowly, gradually, I began to realize what I needed. (In the
language of fly-fishing, 'need' is roughly synonymous with 'want.')
I needed forceps, scissor/pliers, tweezers (no telling what for),
enough leader material to build a hand-tied tapered leader from the
butt down, fingernail clippers with a folding knife blade that said
'Henry's Fork Anglers/Last Chance, Idaho' on them (only a rank
amateur buys his clippers from a drug store), a combination tape
measure and scale, stomach pump, bug net, specimen bottles, fly
boxes, leader stretchers, waterproof match holder, wader patch kit,
flashlight, two types of each fly float and fly sink, and, well . . .

I learned that getting oneself properly outfitted wasn't cheap, or even acceptable in some circles. I was still married to my second wife at the time, and I can recall the long, serious discussions over the kitchen table at two o'clock in the morning over the relative values of three-hundred dollars' worth of fly tackle (plus eighty dollars for a bigger vest to carry it all in) and, say, getting the leak in the roof fixed.

The fact that I am single now only illustrates that a sportsman of my caliber can't possibly live with someone whose ducks aren't in a row. She used to say, 'You never take me anywhere!' and I'd answer calmly, logically, 'I took you fishing just last month.'

A friend once asked, 'How come a guy who dresses in rags and drives a smoky old pickup can afford such snazzy tackle?'

'It should be obvious.'

From STILL WATER ANGLING

BY RICHARD WALKER (1975)

The late Richard Walker was among the most prolific and
influential innovators in the fields of both game and coarse fishing,
and a gifted writer upon almost every aspect of the sport.
Countless advances in tackle, equipment and technique are owed to
his questing mind and capacity for setting his thoughts down
lucidly, while his account below of his capture of the record carp
in 1952 remains a classic of angling literature.

* * *

O N 12TH SEPTEMBER, 1952, PETER THOMAS AND I WENT TO
Redmire.
We left home in a downpour, but by the time we had reached our
destination the sky had cleared and the stars were shining brightly.
It was very cold indeed, but we fished until about 2 a.m., when we
noticed a bank of black cloud coming from the north-west, and
decided to pitch our tent before it began to rain again.

We chose a spot on the west side of the lake, in deference to a
theory I have that when carp have been driven into deep water at
night by lowering temperature, they usually move out of it again in
the early morning on the side which first catches the morning
sunshine. Here we camped, pitching the tent with its open end
about three yards from the water and directly facing it. Between the
tent and the water's edge a large ground-sheet was spread.

Looking across the lake, about a hundred yards wide at this
point, we could see a line of trees, which appeared black as shadows.
To the left, ten yards along the bank, was a clump of weeping
willows, whose branches trailed in the water, and beyond them was
the tough pond-weed of which I spoke when describing the capture
of Maurice Ingham's fish. This extended about twenty yards out
into the lake, as did another bed of the same stuff on the right of

our position. Beyond that, forty yards away, was the dam at the end
of the lake, which runs at right angles to the bank from which we
were fishing. Half-way along the dam were once some chestnut trees,
which have long since been felled, but their stumps still live and a
tangled mass of writhing roots trail in the water. Immediately to our
right, on the bank from which we were fishing, was a mass of
brambles hanging in the water and extending to the bottom,
concealing an undercut bank hollowed-out to a depth of between
three and four feet, a favourite haunt of moorhens and rats.

Having arranged our week-end home, we baited our hooks and
cast out to the edge of the deep water, a few yards beyond the
pond-weed; Peter's to the left and mine only a few yards to the
right where his bait landed. Both baits consisted of balanced paste
and breadcrust on No. 2 hooks which had been carefully sharpened
beforehand; mine was whipped direct to a 12lb. B. S. plaited nylon
line, of which I had 100 yards on a fixed-spool reel. Rods were the
usual Mk IV carp-rods, which have never failed us yet – ten ounces
of hardened split-bamboo can be made to do surprising things.
Electric buzzers were clipped to the lines between butt-rings and
reels, and all was ready for the carp to bite; to attract them, mashed
bread ground-bait was thrown out. By this time, the sky had
clouded over completely, and instead of rain there was a decided
increase in temperature, but the darkness was intense. I cannot
remember ever being out on a blacker night. It was so dark that
even the rats were less active than usual, and all I could see were
the silhouettes of the trees opposite. The lake was completely still,
its surface unbroken by either wind or the movements of fish; and
so it remained, except for one heavy splash far out, and a brief
spell of 'flipping' by very small fish on the surface, until some time
between 4.30 a.m. and 5 a.m. About that time one of the buzzers
sounded, and we were both at the rods at once.

'It's yours,' said Peter. I raised the back of my hand under the
rod to feel if the line was being taken, and felt it creep slowly over
the hairs, an eerie but satisfactory sensation. In went the pick-up; a
pause to make sure the line had been picked up properly, and then
I struck hard and far back. I encountered a solid but living

resistance, and Peter, needing no telling that a fish was hooked, reeled up his line out of the way. I crouched so that I could see the curve of the rod against the sky – even that was difficult in the extreme darkness – and waited on events. I did not want a fresh lively fish brought too soon into the fifteen-yard wide channel between the water-beds, and I determined that if possible the battle should be fought in the deep water beyond.

The fish moved slowly and solidly towards the dam. Every few seconds came a tremendous tug; it felt as if the rod had been struck by a sandbag. As the fish neared the dam, I remembered those chestnut roots. Four pounds or forty, it must not get among them, or all would be lost, so I increased pressure. At first it had no effect; then as I bent the rod more, the efforts of the fish became intensified. I knew only a few yards separated it from disaster, and hung on grimly. The rod bent as never before – I could feel the curve under the corks in my hand; but everything held for the two or three minutes that the fish continued to fight his way towards his refuge. Then, suddenly, he gave it up. He turned and forged into the weed-bed between me and the roots, and I was only just able to keep the line taut. Presently he stopped, and all was solid and immovable.

Peter said, 'Take it easy. Wait and see if he'll move.' I did. Nothing happened. I said, 'I'll try hand-lining.' Peter said, 'All right, but *take it easy*. That's a big fish, you don't want to lose it.'

I had no idea how big a fish it was. I knew it was a good one, but all I could think of then was: 'Maybe another twenty-pounder – I hope!' I pulled off a couple of yards of line, so as to be able to get the rod up quickly if the fish bolted suddenly; then I pointed the rod straight at the fish and began tugging. The first few tugs made no impression; then came a frantic pull, up went the rod, and out went the fish into the deep water

again. I let him go well out, and
then tightened up firmly again,
praying for him to move *left*; and
he did. When he was opposite I
gave him the butt and crammed on
pressure to the limit; and in he
came, grudgingly, pulling and
boring every inch of the way,
but always losing ground, until
at last he came to the surface
and rolled three or four yards out.

Peter was ready with the net, and
as I drew the fish towards it, he switched on the electric lamp. We
saw a great expanse of golden flank as the fish rolled. 'Common
carp,' said Peter. The fish rolled again, then righted itself, and
suddenly, with a last effort, shot towards me, and to the right. I
could do nothing to stop it, and to my horror it crashed through
the fringe of trailing brambles; in the light of the lamp I could see
the swirls as the fish tried to thrust even farther under; but though
I put the rod-point under water and strained it as hard as I dare,
nothing would shift the fish, which eventually settled down into an
immovable sulk.

Peter climbed out to the edge of the overhang and put the big
net, thong down, over the hole in the brambles where the fish had
gone in. Then, feeling carefully down the line with his free hand, he
reached the fish's nose and pulled it round, steering it into the net.
I saw vaguely a commotion; then Peter began to lift. He stuck half-
way and called for me to take his lamp. I slackened the line, put
down the rod and went to his assistance. Once I had the lamp, he
could grasp the mesh of the net, and with a tremendous heave he
swung net and fish up and over the brambles and on to the bank.

We knelt side-by-side looking at it. I knew it was big, and
suddenly it dawned on me it was more than that. It was
tremendous! I cut a stick, notched its end, and with this Peter
extracted the hook which was only lightly lodged in the roof of the
mouth. Then we put the fish in a sack and lifted it on my spring

balance, which goes up to 32lb. The pointer came up against the stop with such a thump that we both knew at once that here was a new record; but we could tell no more; so we tied up the mouth of the sack and lowered it into the water.

Then we re-baited our hooks and cast out again. Peter went into the tent; but I knew I could never sleep, and sat smoking and thinking till dawn. It was then that I resolved that, record or no record, that fish should not be killed. Many, many times I had wondered what I should do if ever I caught a record carp; now I had to decide, and kill it I could not.

At about ten-thirty, I was able to telephone Mr H. F. Vinall, curator of the aquarium at the London Zoo. To cut a long story short, a van containing a vast tub, and two good fellows, who gave up their Saturday afternoon for the purpose, came and fetched it; and it arrived alive and well. I asked that it should be accurately weighed on arrival, which was done, and the weight recorded at 44lb. I thought the sack must have been included at first, but the matter was investigated, and it has now been established that the weight really was 44lb to the dot, without the sack or anything else.

It is now living in a large tank at the Zoo aquarium.

From THE FACE OF ENGLAND

BY EDMUND BLUNDEN (1932)

Edmund Blunden (1896–1974) was a poet, scholar, editor and man of letters. He fought at Ypres and the Somme during the First World War and won a Military Cross for bravery. In later life Blunden was professor of poetry at Oxford University. He wrote several books, including biographies of Leigh Hunt and Shelley, but he was primarily a poet, much of his work having rural themes and natural imagery. A lover of cricket, country life and landscape, it seems only right and fitting to end this anthology with the following almost elegiac extract from *The Face of England*.

* * *

THE JUNE EVENING IS ALMOST OVER. THE ROSY LIGHT FADES FROM the oaks, and from the willows the voices of the doves are ceasing; out of the nettles that hide the angler's lair comes one talking to himself. It seems natural in this light with the bats wheeling capriciously in the air. We follow him and his wicker basket along the footpath separating the wood and weed from plantations of young fruit trees, newly fenced with tall tarred stakes.

His walk, and ours, emerges into a lane, and he goes into a large white house with a quince tree by its gate – outpost to a few thatched cottages, an alehouse, a workshop, and a duck's pond with the ducks asleep on the shore. We envy him the wide diamond window where he will be sitting a little later to enjoy the look and presence of the night.

The time is happy and serene, the darkness not that forbidding shroud which falls so often when there is no moon, but sweetly awake, luminous; the far-stealing dawn seems already to be glancing on the horizon of rounded hills and rising orchards. At times from the woods by the river, or woods by rivers of another world, a sigh passes through the element, and dimly answered by our trees for a brief moment is lessening away towards the horizon. We may fancy in such a night that it is the spirit of the wild cherries among the woods by the river, communing with their kindred sheltered here about the hamlet. The small, child-like complaint of birds awakened by fear is still again; and to us the hawthorn thickets round cattle-waterings far away at the end of the pastures are made as clear as though seen at noonday by the eclogues of nightingales.

Then comes your little suspecting owl to alight on the gate and at last discovers us. The pheasant's clamour, the fox's bark, do not disturb this world of dewy tranquillity. The whistle of the trains on the main line comes transformed into a voice of reverie, the rushing wheels only send us a murmur like the songs of the little waterfall below this gloom of fragrant interweaving boughs.